The Food GARDEN

☆

COMPILED AND EDITED BY MEG HERD

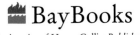

BayBooks

An imprint of HarperCollins*Publishers*

A Bay Books Publication

Bay Books, an imprint of HarperCollins Publishers
25 Ryde Road, Pymble, Sydney, NSW 2073, Australia
31 View Road, Glenfield, Auckland 10, New Zealand

First published in Australia in 1994

National Library of Australia
Cataloguing-in-Publication data:

  The Food garden
  ISBN 1 86378 115 3
  1. Vegetable gardening — Australia. 2. Fruit-culture — Australia.
  I. Herd, Meg.
635

Front cover photograph by Ivy Hansen
Printed in Singapore

7 6 5 4 3 2 1
98 97 96 95 94

CONTENTS

THE KITCHEN GARDEN ◆ 4

A guide to growing vegetables and fruit in your backyard; information on soils, soil preparation, watering, drainage, composting, companion planting, nutrients and organic growing; propagating plants from seeds; seasonal planting guide; growing food-crops in containers.

VEGETABLES ◆ 26

Alphabetical listing of vegetables under the following categories: buds, bulbs, flowers, fruits, leaf crops, pods and seeds, roots, stems, tubers, Asian vegetables. All listings provide information on cultivation, growing conditions and varieties.

FRUIT CROPS ◆ 76

Alphabetical listing of the fruit crops which are easy to grow at home, categorised under berry fruits and fruit of the vine.

PESTS, DISEASES AND WEEDS ◆ 86

How to keep your food-crop garden healthy and productive; chemical and organic alternatives for controlling pests and diseases; pest and disease control chart; information on weed control.

THE KITCHEN GARDEN

Growing your own food crops and supplying the kitchen with fresh produce can be a most rewarding pastime, giving great personal satisfaction. In order to meet the household's vegetable needs, a gardener can harvest kilos of healthy crops from a well-managed garden. An efficient grower who keeps beds in order, removes weeds, keeps pests and diseases at bay, maintains tools, adds organic matter, gives at least one complete fertilising per year plus an occasional liming and buys certified seed can produce clean, top-quality vegetables.

VEGETABLES AND HERBS MIX WELL IN THE FOOD-CROP GARDEN.

Home-grown crops are undoubtedly fresher and more flavoursome than their commercially available counterparts and the cook will certainly appreciate having produce of such quality to work with in the kitchen.

The style of food-crop garden depends in part on the amount of space the grower is prepared to allot to vegetables. If relegated to the back garden they will probably share space with a garage or garden shed, a drying area, pool, the occasional tree, a child's play area or they may be restricted to scanty borders around a lawn. Space-saving ideas include growing attractive vegetables in pots and tubs or as a feature in a herbaceous border. A drift of rainbow chard, silverbeet or a border of parsley suits this function well. Where appropriate vegetables can be grown in front borders in conjunction with flowering annuals. Flowers and vegetables both respond to good gardening habits, and where one can be grown successfully so can the other. Vine crops such as passionfruit or kiwi fruit can be trained over a pergola just as easily as purely ornamental vines but also provide food in addition to function and beauty.

However, if food-crop growing is to be undertaken seriously, enough sunny space will have to be rendered up and devoted to the task of cropping in order to supply a fair proportion of the household's vegetable requirements.

Traditional vegetable gardening involves a portion of an allotment being extensively and continually cropped. The same area may be cropped up to five times annually and unless nutrients are replaced the soil will become impoverished. So to become a successful grower of food-crops there must be a sympathetic relationship with the earth. The condition of soil plays a crucial role in the production and quality of food.

For a food-crop gardener a knowledge of the soil and the below-ground biology of plants and other living organisms is vital to success.

A grower of vegetables and fruits has sovereignty over a plot. He or she may neglect plants' requirements and consequently rob the soil of every vestige of essential minerals, or the grower can renew and invigorate the soil by regular fertilising and additions of organic matter, cultivation, and crop rotation.

Preliminary tasks such as site selection, considering sun, shade and shelter, making provision for a watering system, marking out and digging the beds, and adding organic matter and fertiliser, must be undertaken prior to crop selection, raising seeds or planting.

An understanding of climatic limitations is also important to growing food-crops.

Home-garden vegetables can be grown in all climatic zones but essential to their culture is a knowledge of the special requirements for cold and warm temperatures; many vegetable crops fail because they are planted out of season.

All cool-season vegetables grow best at temperatures 10–20°C or lower and are frost-resistant. Broad beans, broccoli, Brussels sprouts, cauliflower, kohlrabi, onions, peas, spinach, turnips and swedes belong to this group. Sow or transplant them in late summer, autumn or early winter to grow during the cooler months. Brussels sprouts, cauliflower and spinach are difficult to grow in warm temperate, northern climates because the temperature, even in winter, is not sufficiently cold.

Warm-season vegetables grow best at high temperatures (20–35°C) and tolerate even higher ones. They grow poorly at low temperatures and are frost-susceptible. Beans, capsicum, eggplant, okra, potato, rosella, sweet corn, sweet potato, tomato and the creeping vine-like cucurbits, such as pumpkin, are warm-season crops. In mild and cold climates, they should be planted in spring or early summer to grow during the warmer months. In tropical and subtropical climates, many can be grown throughout the year. Choko, eggplant, okra, rosella and sweet potato are difficult to grow in cold climates because the summer season is too short.

A third group of vegetables have intermediate temperature requirements and grow best at 15–25°C. In this category are beetroot, cabbage, carrot, celery, endive, leek, lettuce, parsnip, radish, rhubarb, silver beet and spring onions. Radish and spring onions have a very short growing period and can be planted at any time of the year in all climatic zones. Other vegetables in this group, especially root crops — beetroot, carrot and parsnip — may 'bolt' or run to seed if sown too late in autumn or winter or too early in spring. Silver beet may do this too.

Some varieties of cabbage and lettuce will run to seed if

Garden Fresh

Vegetables from the garden can be brought to the table in optimum condition if they are:
- Picked before full maturity.
- Prepared with minimum delay after harvest.
- Washed, not soaked, before preparation.
- Peeled only where necessary.
- Chopped as little as possible before cooking if the cooking liquid is not to be consumed.
- Microwaved or steamed with very little water.
- Not salted until almost cooked.
- Never cooked with bicarbonate of soda.
- Cooked for the shortest period to bring them to 'crunch' tenderness.
- Dried out by shaking the drained pot over heat.

sown during warm weather, so it is important to select sure-heading varieties for growing in summer.

Having regard to all the preliminary considerations the food-crop grower is then ready to select varieties suited to the climate and the household's preference and in time will be bringing an overflowing barrow-load of vegetables to the kitchen door. He or she is going to be that much healthier and that much more in pocket than their non-gardening counterpart!

Planning and Preparing the Site

SITE SELECTION

When choosing a site for the food-crop garden keep in mind that it must have sufficient sun (4–5 hours daily), preferably in the morning.

Before laying down the garden, plot the shade outline thrown by neighbouring buildings, fences, shrubs or trees throughout the year. Long autumn and winter shadows make permanently cold ground. Endeavour to place growing areas outside these shade areas.

A northeasterly or easterly aspect for the food-crop garden is preferred. Siting garden beds at right angles to the axis of the sun, running crop rows north and south, will allow the sun's rays to penetrate along the rows. Shading is kept to a minimum and the soil is consequently warmer. If the site slopes from north to south, run broad beds east to west and plant a number of short rows across them.

In siting the beds look also for protection from harsh winds, street pollution and an overdose of sun. In summer the wind and heat can do a great deal of damage to young plants, so a hedge or makeshift windbreak on the westerly side will certainly help if the site is exposed. Fruit trees grow quickly and are ideal for providing protection during the hot months, or artificial hedges can be made from tan bark, tea-tree or lattice. Permanent windbreaks can be erected, however, solid walls can cause air turbulence. Keep the vegetable garden away from large trees, as roots will cause problems later when the vegetables need to be watered constantly. Ideally, the area for the vegetable garden should be close to the kitchen so it is easy to venture outside and pick vegetables for dinner or salad garnishes.

Decide on the size of your vegetable beds. A family of two adults and two children can be substantially provided for from an intensively cropped area of about 10 m x 5 m. A family of two adults and four children can also be provided for from this area, but with less variety of vegetables as a larger volume of main crops will be needed.

If there are no water taps in the vegetable garden area, it is wise to have plumbing done before the beds are made up so that they will not be disturbed when installing the pipes. Although garden hoses can be lengthened at will, it is much

easier to manage a short length of hose from a conveniently placed tap than to drag hoses any distance.

Securing the whole garden with proper fencing for protection from unwanted animals will pay dividends. Birds can be a nuisance and wire-netting canopies can be erected over vegetable rows. However, birds eat insects so consider this benefit before forcing them to stay away.

Finally, as garden soils will need regeneration by the addition of peat, loam, sand or manure, arrange for truck or barrow access in the area. The average pathway should be 40–50 cm wide which gives a comfortable walking area, enough space to kneel and weed, and sufficient width to wheel a barrow along.

Make access paths in wearable materials (gravel, paving or concrete) which will stand up to heavy wheelbarrow traffic. If turf is retained on paths, mower-strips should be cemented in so that one pass with the mower gives a clean and complete cut.

Drainage

Drainage must be attended to prior to undertaking any bed or site preparation in the food-crop garden. Waterlogged soil spells instant disaster for vegetable culture. Methods must be devised to drain away surplus water prior to beds being laid out.

By far the best method is to lay agricultural pipes below the surface of the soil in trenches 30–60 cm deep through any saturated area, falling to a soakage pit at a lower level. Consult the local authorities as to disposal from this point.

The introduction of flexible, perforated plastic drainpipe (slotted polythene) has all but made other drainage materials obsolete. It is available in long lengths and is light and easy to install. It is corrugated and goes around curves. Place the pipe in the trench then cover with gravel. Joints are made by splitting one end and inserting the split end into the other section. If required, branch lines can also be laid.

All that is necessary to improve drainage in very small areas is a rubble drain set at a low enough level and leading

---

Siting

In the siting of a food-crop garden consider:
A size to suit your needs.
Penetration of light and exposure to sun.
Access and upkeep.
Drainage.
Proximity to water.
Protection from wind.

into a gravel-filled sump at the lowest point in the garden. Surface drains can also be used to divert water, taking it across the top of a slope, as well as collecting it on the way down.

These are permanent ways to drain garden soil. If investing in agricultural pipes or rubble drains is not warranted, build raised beds 15–20 cm above the surrounding level enclosed with railroad sleepers, bricks or concrete edging, and fill with topsoil over a gravel base. Provide weep holes for drainage.

PREPARING THE BED

An essential part of productive fruit and vegetable growing is preparing the soil thoroughly over two to three weeks before planting. Start by removing all the weeds, surface rubbish, stones, and broken bricks or rubble which may be in the soil. Then turn the soil with a spade or shovel to a depth of 20–25 cm, leaving the soil in large clods. Heavy soil may need a mattock to break the surface before using the spade. Do not dig the soil if it is too wet; the ideal moisture level is when the soil crumbles easily in the hand.

If the pH (see page 16) is below 6.0, sprinkle a generous covering of agricultural lime over the soil and leave for a week before checking again. A reading of 6.5 is ideal for most vegetables. Cover the dug area with garden compost, mushroom compost or well-rotted animal manure to a depth of 5–8 cm and work into the soil. Keep working the soil with a fork to kill emerging weeds and to establish a light, crumbly structure. Finally, rake to level the soil and leave a fine surface on the bed ready for planting out seeds or seedlings.

PRUNED AND STAKED TOMATO PLANTS WILL PRODUCE A HEAVIER YIELD THAN THOSE GROWN ON BUSHES.

CROP AND BED DESIGN

Once the area is prepared, make a planting design. It is best to grow annual vegetables in one area, so consider the length of time that each plant takes to mature. Beans and lettuce are in the ground for three months; peas — four to five months; cabbages, cauliflowers, broccoli and Brussels sprouts — four to six months; potatoes — six months; and carrots, parsnips, leeks, onions and many other root crops — up to ten months. The vine crops like cucumber, melon, zucchini, pumpkin and squash may be in the ground from late winter to the following autumn and take up a lot of room with their sprawling habit. They can be trained on trellises to encourage them to spread upwards instead of outwards. Tomatoes are also in the ground for a long time depending on the variety grown. Save space by staking two plants at a time and keeping them well tied up.

Before planting any vegetables, find out their maximum growing height and plan your garden accordingly. Do not plant a row of lettuces down the centre of a bed and then plant a border of sweet corn. Always plant tall vegetables such as broad beans, sweet corn and tomatoes on the southern side of low growing crops to prevent shading.

Also, grow vegetables that will survive in the local climate, and know their seasons and the maximum and minimum temperatures they tolerate; it is no good hoping that frost will not kill early tomatoes or the heat will not affect the flowering of Brussels sprouts. Finally, choose vegetables that everyone in the household likes to eat; grow small quantities at a time to avoid an unnecessary glut and waste; and select those vegetables which are difficult to obtain or expensive to buy locally. Crops which are considered to be permanent because they occupy a space for three years or more, such as strawberries, asparagus or rhubarb, are best not planted in a vegetable patch but positioned somewhere else in the garden. Some will fit quite attractively into a herbaceous border, in clumps near fences, walls or under trees.

CROP ROTATION

Crop rotation means the same sort of crop is not grown in the same bed twice running. Since vegetables are classified according to their families, one rule of rotation is that no crop should follow another of the same family in the same bed.

Closely related crops generally use the same nutrients from the soil in the same proportions. Accordingly, when the same or related crops are grown in succession, there is a tendency for these food materials to become heavily depleted in the soil, and yields are gradually reduced until eventually crops can fail.

In addition, the proliferation of many soil-borne diseases

Crop Families

BOTANICAL FAMILY NAME	INDIVIDUAL CROPS
Amaryllidaceae	Chives, garlic, leek, onion, shallot, Japanese bunching onion
Apiaceae	Carrot, celery, parsnip
Asteraceae	Cardoon, chicory, endive, globe artichoke, Jerusalem artichoke, lettuce
Brassicaceae	Broccoli, Brussels sprouts, cabbage, cauliflower, kale, kohlrabi, mustard, radish, swede, turnip, bok choy, Chinese cabbage
Chenopodiaceae	Beetroot, silver beet, spinach
Convolvulaceae	Sweet potato
Cucurbitaceae	Choko, cucumber, marrow, melon, zucchini, pumpkin, squash
Dilleniaceae	Kiwi fruit
Fabaceae	Peas, beans
Lilliaceae	Asparagus
Malvaceae	Okra, rosella
Passifloraceae	Passionfruit
Poaceae	Sweet corn
Polygonaceae	Rhubarb
Rosaceae	Strawberry, raspberry
Saxifragaceae	Gooseberry
Solanaceae	Cape gooseberry, capsicum, eggplant, potato, tomato
Zingiberaceae	Ginger

means there is much greater danger of a crop being affected if it is the same as or closely related to the previous crop.

With crops that are particularly prone to soil-borne disease (potatoes, strawberries and tomatoes) a period of at least two, and preferably three or even four years should elapse before the same crop is again raised in the same bed.

It is also possible that where there is continuous cropping of the one type or family in one area, a build-up of harmful insect populations can occur.

Crop rotation does not automatically guarantee a rich yield; if other essential factors are absent, rotation will have no benefit. For example, in soils that have not been properly limed or in soils that lack essential nutrients mere rotation will do little to improve crop yields. There is one notable exception. When the soil deficiency is in nitrogen, there will often be a marked increase in yield in the crop following a legume. Other things being equal, when a legume (peas, beans) is used in a rotation, most crops following it will definitely benefit. Only unusual adverse factors such as lack of some essential element or exceptional climatic conditions will negate the benefit.

CROP ROTATION EXAMPLES

To carry out crop rotation properly, it is necessary to keep a plan of the garden and a diary in which planting records are kept, preferably noting when each crop was planted, into which plot it went and when the harvest was completed. Such events are difficult to remember as the seasons progress.

Taking into account seasonal sowing times and local conditions and assuming the food-crop garden is divided into four plots, begin plot 1 with a heavy-feeding leaf crop like cabbage. If acidic soil prevails, lime the bed prior to planting and add a heavy ration of composted cow manure and complete fertiliser. When the cabbage is harvested, the heavy manuring for the previous crop is ideal for a root crop which must not have fresh manure. Turnip, swede and radish are in the same family as cabbage, so avoid these roots. A suitable choice would be beetroot or carrots.

When this root crop is out, the bed will not have been manured for the last crop so another gross-feeder crop is now possible. As a root crop was previously cultivated, a fruit crop such as tomato, would be a logical choice. After the tomatoes are over, peas or broad beans could be grown, followed by lettuce.

In plot 2 the rotation could be eggplant, beetroot, lettuce, French beans, turnip; and in plot 3 cauliflower, potatoes, cucumber, peas and tomatoes. Plot 4 might be strawberries, which would be in until the runners were lifted a year later; thereafter, you might plant swedes, silver beet, French beans, and onions. In all rotations try to include one of the legumes at least once every four or five rounds.

Some crops, like the strawberries of plot 4, are in the ground for many months, and some, such as asparagus and rhubarb, are in the ground for even longer. Rotation in the ordinary sense is then impossible and it will be necessary to feed the ground regularly if yields are to be kept up.

COMPANION PLANTING

Companion plants are those which are mutually compatible. One plant near another may provide needed shade, such as tall-growing corn protecting the cucurbits (melons, zucchinis, pumpkins and squash) with light shade. A crop may have a strong root system which enables the soil to be beneficially loosened, or may repel insects which would normally be troublesome to the other species. If nasturtiums are planted near broccoli, for example, the broccoli will probably be free of aphids. Conversely, garlic, onion or shallots planted near peas and beans will inhibit their grow.

Chives repel a great many inspects and diseases when sown near other plants; they also have a favourable effect on the growth of carrots. In fact carrots are said to increase in girth if planted near any of the onion family.

Other plants have decided effects on insect and animal life. By growing celery near cabbages and cauliflowers, the white butterfly is repelled. Aromatic herbs such as rosemary, mint and thyme are also effective insect repellents, especially for cabbage pests. If carrots are planted close to sage and rosemary these herbs protect them from the carrot fly. Rows of basil intercropped with tomatoes will keep the tomatoes safe from insects.

Leguminous plants (peas, beans) which bring nitrogenous compounds to other plants through the soil can do this through companion plantings as well as crop rotation.

Companion planting is a wide field of interest for the home gardener. Keep the following points in mind when implementing a companion planting regime.

A plant which needs ample sunlight may provide a harmonious balance with a smaller, semi-shade loving species. Deep-rooted plants will open up the soil for shallow rooted ones. Heavy-feeding plants should be followed by light feeders or legumes to enrich the soil. Herbs can be used widely both for their insect-repellent properties and for their beneficial effect on the growth of many vegetable crops.

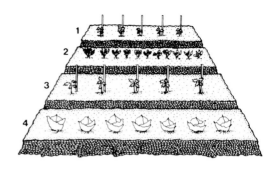

INTERCROPPING UTILISES A SMALL AREA TO THE FULLEST EXTENT. INTERPLANTING CROPS WHICH ARE KNOWN TO BE COMPATIBLE MAY RESULT IN A RICHER YIELD. 1 TOMATOES; 2 RADISHES; 3 TOMATOES; 4 LETTUCES

Soil

Assessing the physical condition of the soil is one of the first matters to claim a food-crop gardener's attention. Once aware of the basic constitution of garden soil, it is possible to improve it to a condition where it will grow virtually anything.

It is sometimes thought that the individual vegetable species need different soil types, that is, that root vegetables require different soils from leaf vegetables. But quality vegetables can be produced as easily from acidic coastal soils as they can from alkaline inland clays and loams. There are good soils and there are difficult soils, but when it comes to growing food it is all a matter of providing the plant roots with the essential substances they require to produce healthy crops.

SOIL TYPES

All soils are made up of different-sized particles categorised as sand, silt and clay. The relative proportions of each of these particles determines the texture of a soil.

If soil has little body and falls loosely apart when handled it may be termed sand, although it may incorporate small amounts of silt and fibrous matter. Loam is recognisably dark because of its content of decayed vegetable matter, but it also may contain sand, silt and clay. The fine nature of silt causes it to powder when crumbled. Clay, especially if damp, is waxy, heavy and cold. When dry, clay is likely to be stone-hard and impossible to crumble by hand. All these soils need one another in differing proportions to mix to a perfect soil.

Perfect soil, were it to be found, would be comprised of clay and silt particles each so fine as to be invisible to the naked eye; sand particles large enough to be recognisable; humus so composted by time that it looks like a friable chocolate filling; and many large pieces of vegetable matter of more recent origin; each in a proportion making a whole that may be termed 'loam'. Such balanced soil is a gardener's dream — it rarely exists. Inferior soils, however, can be improved over a period of time.

Companion Planting Chart

FOOD-CROP	SYMPATHETIC PLANTS	ANTIPATHETIC PLANTS
Asparagus	Parsley, tomato	
Beans	Carrot, cucumber, turnip, celery, eggplant	Garlic, onion
Beetroot	Cabbage, lettuce	Climbing and bush beans
Broccoli	Onion	Tomato, strawberry
Brussels sprouts	Potato	Strawberry
Cabbage	Corn, herbs (rosemary, mint, thyme) with scent to repel cabbage pests	Strawberry, climbing bean, tomato
Capsicum	Carrot, onion	
Carrot	Onion, lettuce, peas, chives, (sage and rosemary protect against carrot fly)	Potato, kohlrabi, cabbage
Cauliflower	Onion, basil, thyme, sage	Strawberry, tomato
Celery	Leek, tomato, beans	
Corn	Broad beans, peas, cucumber, melon, potato	
Cucumber	Corn, cabbage, radish, onion	Aromatic herbs, potato
Eggplant	Beans	Onion, garlic, potato
Endive	Carrot, strawberry, cabbage, beetroot, radish, cucumber	
Kohlrabi	Beetroot, onion, cucumber, thyme	Tomato, strawberry, climbing beans, capsicum
Lettuce	Carrot, strawberry, cabbage, beetroot, radish, cucumber	
Onion	All brassicas, strawberry, lettuce, tomato	Beans, peas
Peas	Early potato, sweet corn, beans, turnip, radish, carrot, cucumber	Onion, garlic, shallot, strawberry
Potato	Corn, beans, cabbage, peas, strawberry, celery	Tomato, pumpkin, cucumber, raspberry, Brussels sprouts
Pumpkin	Corn	Potato
Radish	Peas, cucumber, lettuce, squash, kohlrabi, tomato	
Silver beet	Beetroot, onion	
Spinach	Strawberry	
Strawberry	Beans, lettuce, spinach	Cabbage, cauliflower, Brussels sprouts
Tomato	Cabbage, carrot, radish, asparagus, peas, celery, sage, basil, parsley	Potato, kohlrabi, fennel
Turnip	Peas, French beans	Mustard
Zucchini	Beans, radish, sweet corn	

SAND

Sand is the largest-sized grain in soil. It is largely of quartz origin, sterile in nature, porous and loose and cannot retain moisture. Its bacterial life is nonexistent and yet it is warm and well aerated. It is therefore an important addition to denser soils where it makes an immediate and permanent improvement to the soil structure. But of itself, it quickly loses water, minerals and organic mulches or manures. Its composition is such that it cannot retain them at a level useable by short-rooted crops. But a mixture of sand and vermiculite makes a satisfactory seed-raising medium because of its excellent drainage and sterile nature.

To improve sandy soil, add organic matter, animal manures, spent mushroom compost, leafmould and garden compost.

All organic materials will eventually decompose so they must be renewed periodically, especially in a vegetable garden which is cultivated regularly.

LOAM

Loam soil is the ideal type, although it rarely occurs naturally. Its particles are next in size to those of sand and are larger than those of silt or clay. A rich loam soil contains clay particles, coarse sand and organic particles of old and new origin. Its structure is loose and finely crumbly. A friable soil does not form a crust or cake; water enters freely and drains easily. Air- and water-holding capacity, heat absorption, ease of root penetration and uptake of plant nutrients are all at optimum levels. To maintain these ideal conditions moderate moisture and continued supplies of humus are necessary.

SILT

A fine-particled soil with a high proportion of clay, silt is deposited in position by water action. Because it has been transported and then set down by water it is even in structure and rich in minerals leached from soils at higher levels.

Silt is the main constituent of alluvial valley soils and river flats. It becomes a manageable garden soil with the addition of sand and organic matter. Clenched in the hand when damp, it has a tendency to clump together into small lumps. When dry these same clumps can be compressed into powder.

CLAY

Clay occurs in all colours and consistencies. When wet it is heavy and plastic with trapped water. It is equally unworkable when completely dry, for then it becomes stonelike. The fine, food-finding root hairs of foraging plants cannot penetrate clay.

The small air spaces in clay readily become waterlogged. Owing to poor aeration and coldness when wet, it has a low bacterial count despite its good mineral constitution. Clay is totally unworkable when wet and considerable damage can be done to the soil's tilth by endeavouring to cultivate it in this condition, as it will wedge into granite-like lumps. When just moist, clay clumps can be smashed into smaller particles with the edge of the spade, but a fine tilth is only possible when structural improvement has been undertaken.

To improve clay soils add organic matter in substantial quantities. Sand may also be added but massive amounts will be required.

STONY SOILS

Areas quite unsuitable for gardening are best dealt with by using raised beds filled with imported soil, not forgetting to provide adequate drainage.

SOIL MANAGEMENT

Whatever the original nature of the garden soil it is the food-crop gardener's task to maintain or improve its physical condition.

By mixing together soils of varying particle sizes, a growing medium is obtained which is neither so loose that

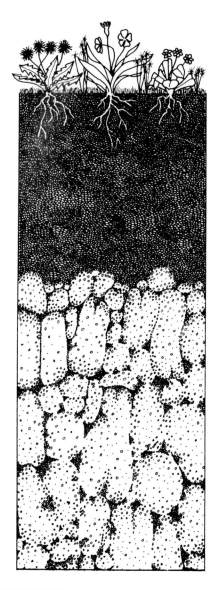

SOIL IMPROVEMENT
IN CLAY SOILS, A THIN LAYER OF TOPSOIL ALONE IS INSUFFICIENT. THE DENSE CLAY NEEDS LIGHTENING WITH ADDITIONS OF ORGANIC MATTER, COMPOST AND SAND.

it cannot retain water nor so close that it cannot retain air. By introducing large amounts of well-composted organic matter into the soil, the micro-organic community will be encouraged to develop to the point where it begins to convert minerals into plant foods. At the same time the structure of the soil becomes more friable and manageable. Aeration and percolation are also improved in soils with a high organic content.

Soils absorb nutrients in solution. These nutrients are provided by decomposed organic matter or chemical fertilisers. The soil must open to enable the roots to penetrate it easily in search of food and water, and the elements must be present to be taken up by the plant as ions with the water. To be capable of supporting a series of garden food crops, your garden soil should be of the best structure possible using clay, sand, loam and organic compost; well granulated and of open structure; able to support a high micro-organic population; and able to hold the mineral nutrients provided.

Organic matter is the key to healthy soil. What has been taken out of the soil must be returned. In natural environments where plant material is allowed to mature, wither and die without interference, the detritus settles on top of the soil and its food elements are returned to the earth. Each seed is capable of increasing vital soil foods many times over by virtue of the size of the plant it produces. The minute animal life of the earth carries particles from the plant detritus back into the soil in an endless cycle. Micro-organic life forms work incessantly at converting these materials back into plant foods. All this action comes to a halt when food crops are harvested and taken away without returning a comparable amount of plant food to the soil. For the food-crop gardener the lesson to be learned is to emulate nature — recycle, compost and return it to the soil.

Nutrients

ORGANIC MATERIALS

Animal manure and green manure crops add nutrients to the soil while improving its structure. Animal manure is slower acting than chemical fertiliser as it must be broken down by soil bacteria before the nutrients can be used by plants. Manures are preferred for feeding delicate, shallow-rooted plants which do not take kindly to the more concentrated and quicker acting inorganic fertilisers. As organic manures contain only small amounts of plant nutrients they must be applied in large quantities, are bulky, and therefore more difficult to transport and handle than inorganic fertilisers. The effectiveness of animal manure is spread over a longer period than that of chemical fertilisers, which are more readily absorbed by plants.

Compost fresh animal manure before spreading it over the garden bed, as the heat generated during decomposition destroys the viability of weed seeds. Fresh manure will burn young plants if it is applied too thickly and too close to the plant. Composting under cover for several weeks or months breaks the manure down to a useable consistency and allows the heat to dissipate. Horse, cow, sheep and poultry manures, although varying in nutrient content, are valuable soil improvers.

A green manure crop grown on the site for this purpose should be dug into the bed. Beans, peas, lupins, wheat and rye make reliable green crop manures. The legume crops serve to inoculate the soil with nitrogen-building bacteria. As well as improving soil structure, all green manures return to the soil the minerals they have taken up while growing. It is important that a green manure crop be dug in while it is juicy and growing strongly. Once it has made tough stalks it takes longer to decompose and may actually check the growth of a subsequent crop, as the micro-organisms breaking down the compost will use available soil nitrogen which the plants require.

FARMYARD MANURES The nutrient value of animal manures varies considerably with the animal, its age, its diet and the amount of straw or litter mixed with the manure. Stall-fed animals or those grazing on well-fertilised, rich pasture will excrete manure comparatively high in nutrients; conversely the manure from poorly fed animals will be comparatively low in nutrients. Its nutrient status is also affected by how fresh or old it is and how it is stored. Manure is not stable and on decomposition loses nitrogen and becomes less bulky, especially if stored in loose heaps in the open where it is subject to leaching by rain.

Generally, it is best to dig fresh manure into the soil but this should be done some time before the bed is to be planted, especially when using fowl manure, because in the decomposition process nitrogen in the manure is the converted to ammonia which may damage germinating seeds and young plants. Manure with a lot of litter mixed with it may cause a temporary nitrogen shortage because the bacteria engaged in decomposition of the litter are using this element, making it unavailable to the plants.

Animal manures supply more nitrogen (which encourages foliage) than phosphorus or potassium, (see pages 15 and 16 on plant food elements) so the lavish use of these manures alone may lead to excessive vegetative growth and poor development of roots, tubers, flowers, fruits and seeds. Where large quantities of animal manure are used, add phosphorus in the form of superphosphate (four parts) and potassium as potassium sulphate (one part) applied at the rate of 100 g per square metre.

Horse manure is fibrous, dry and open. It breaks down quickly releasing heat and nitrogen, and is favoured for use on heavy soils. Cow manure is finely divided and more compact. Breaking down slowly, it is useful on sandy soils

Making a Compost Heap

There are many types of compost bin on the market which can be purchased at garden centres or local councils. All do a relatively good job of producing rich, productive humus if a suitable range of refuse materials is used and adequate time is allowed for the process of decomposition to work.

Alternatively, a compost stack can be made — a three-bin system is the ideal method as one heap can be built up while another is being turned and the other is maturing.

To make compost, stack alternate layers of organic materials and soil; each layer 10–15 cm deep. The first layer may be of disease-free plant residue after harvest. Chop all coarse material with a sharp spade before putting down the first layer. It is important to chop up and reduce in size woody or tough matter so that all materials will decompose evenly.

Place a 15 cm layer of lawn clippings on top and sprinkle with a handful of agricultural lime, general fertiliser or superphosphate.

Place a 15 cm layer of open-textured rich soil over the vegetable matter and repeat the layers until all materials are incorporated. It is important to keep the layers more or less even in depth and level. Continually supply the growing stack with household refuse such as tea leaves, coffee grounds, vegetable and fruit peelings, eggshells, shredded newspaper, ash from wood fires and the like, but do not include bulbous weeds such as oxalis, weeds with seed heads, invasive grass runners like kikuyu, or diseased plants. Straw, lucerne hay and animal manures are all valuable additions.

Do not use great quantities of any one material such as autumn leaves. Disperse these throughout the heap but avoid getting the materials out of balance. Providing rich soil is used in the layers, enough bacterial starters will be introduced to get the stack decomposing.

The stack's position should be a warm, sheltered one, not a cold dark corner. It must be well aerated. If the walls of the bay are of solid construction, make sure there are plenty of air holes or spaces left between the bricks at the bottom of the side walls. The stack should also be protected from leaching rain. Cover with hessian or other porous materials to reduce leaching and leave the stack for four to six months to do its work, damping down with the hose occasionally.

Turning the stack with a garden fork and bringing the outside material to the inside will hasten decomposition but if you have a large micro-organic population, proper aeration and dampness, the stack should break down readily without turning. If stable sweepings, fowl, sheep or cow manure are available, use them liberally in the compost stack.

Decomposed compost (humus) can be dug into a bed about to be planted, but partially decomposed compost can only be used as a mulch or dug into a bed which will lie fallow for a few weeks (the length of time depends on the weather: the higher the temperature, the shorter the time).

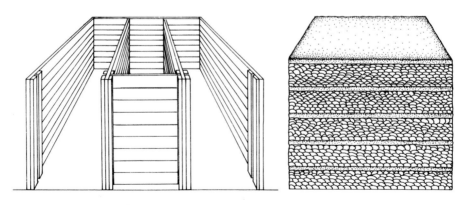

MAKING COMPOST
A THREE-BIN SYSTEM IS IDEAL FOR MAKING COMPOST, ALLOWING ONE HEAP TO BE BUILT UP, WHILE ONE IS TURNED AND THE LAST IS MATURING. MAKE BINS APPROXIMATELY 2 M LONG BY 1.5 M HIGH, WITH REMOVABLE FRONT BOARDS TO FACILITATE WORKING.
CROSS SECTION SHOWS HOW 15 CM LAYERS OF GARDEN REFUSE AND KITCHEN WASTE ARE ALTERNATED WITH 2 CM LAYERS OF SOIL.

because of its long-lasting effect. Sheep manure is drier than other animal manures and is richer in nitrogen than both horse and cow manure. The excrement is in pellet form which makes it easy to spread but it breaks down quickly. Pig manure is similar to cow manure but is heavier, slower acting and longer lasting. When pigs are housed and fed concentrated rations, their manure is often higher in nutrients than cow manure.

Fowl manure is the most valuable not only because the birds are fed a rich diet but also because urine is mixed with the solid excrement. Dried and pelletised fowl manure is very concentrated, so use it in moderate amounts.

Most animal manures can be spread on the soil at rates up to 3 kg per square metre; fowl manure at half that rate. Although animal manures supply useful quantities of nutrients, their greatest contribution to soils is their effect on soil structure. After decomposition, the residual humus particles act as soil colloids and attract and hold plant nutrients on their surface. On heavy soils, humus helps to bind the clay and silt particles together and so improves aeration and drainage. On sandy soils, moisture-holding capacity is increased.

ANIMAL BY-PRODUCTS   Blood and bone contains 4–8 per cent nitrogen and a smaller percentage of phosphorus. Some brands of blood and bone have been fortified with urea to increase their nitrogen content.

Bone dust contains 1–4 per cent nitrogen and somewhat more phosphorus. It is useful where a slow release of phosphorus, especially for container grown plants, is required.

Dried blood (blood meal) contains 10–14 per cent nitrogen and is a good source of this element for leafy plants. The nitrogen breaks down more rapidly than in other animal by-products. Dried blood contains no phosphorus or potassium so should generally be used in conjunction with superphosphate and potassium sulphate to give a balanced NPK (nitrogen, phosphorus, potassium) ratio.

Hoof and horn meal contains 7–15 per cent nitrogen but is slower acting than dried blood. It is useful for vegetables like tomatoes and capsicums which bear over a long period. Hoof and horn contains negligible amounts of phosphorus and potassium so should be mixed with superphosphate and potassium sulphate to provide a balanced base fertiliser. Liquid fish emulsion contains fish meal fortified with other inorganic ingredients to balance the NPK value.

PLANT WASTES   Garden compost is a convenient and inexpensive way of converting waste plant material and kitchen scraps into organic matter and humus. Spent mushroom compost has a nutrient value comparable with that of horse or cow manure. It may be dug into the soil during preparation of vegetable beds. Leafmould consists of decayed leaves which readily break into small particles through which the roots of plants can forage freely. Leaf-

All garden refuse may be added to compost excepting diseased plants, and weeds with tough underground bulbs like onion weed, oxalis and nut grass.

mould alone is high in carbon and low in nitrogen, so may cause a nitrogen deficiency when large quantities are dug into the soil.

For food-crop gardeners who live by the sea, seaweed is a useful product. It contains small quantities of potassium, calcium and trace elements but is low in nitrogen and phosphorus. Seaweed is best chopped finely and added to the compost heap where it breaks down fairly rapidly.

As we have noted, green manure cropping is a productive way of adding nutrients and bulk into the food-crop garden. Legume crops, which through their association with root nodule bacteria add nitrogen to the soil, are often preferred over other cereal crops. Lupins, vetches, field peas and tick beans are also suitable crops. Sow in autumn, either alone or mixed with cereals, and dig into the soil just after flowering commences in spring.

Summer-growing green manure crops are sown in spring and incorporated in late summer or early autumn. Japanese millet, Sudan grass or forage sorghum make for quick, leafy growth, and the best of the summer legumes are cow peas and lab lab bean.

Before digging in the crops, water them if the soil is very dry. If the crop is tall, flatten it and chop the material with a spade. After digging in, keep the soil damp but not wet for a few weeks. Then dig the soil over again and the bed should be ready to use in three or four weeks.

If there is any sign of yellowing (nitrogen deficiency) in the following crop, it indicates that the green manure was not fully decomposed. Correct this by applying a nitrogen fertiliser as a side dressing.

CHEMICAL FERTILISERS

MAJOR ELEMENTS   The three major plant food elements available from fertilisers are nitrogen (N), phosphorus (P) and potassium (K). These three major elements are expressed as a ratio (NPK) and are listed on the fertiliser package.

Nitrogen's most obvious effect is the promotion of leaf growth and healthy green foliage colour. Plants require nitrogen to increase their leaf and stem area. When a plant is denied nitrogen its foliage will yellow and the leaves fall. Too much nitrogen has catastrophic results: floppy growth, lowered disease resistance, diminished harvest and liability to damage by cold.

Phosphorus in a plant promotes maturity by stimulating flowering and makes for an extended harvest. It also aids the development of vigorous root structure. When available to a plant in the right amount it increases disease resistance and the ability to withstand drought. A lack of phosphorus shows up in dull bronzy leaves and may also cause fruit drop.

Potassium is essential for the formation of healthy cells in the plant body. It balances nitrogen and phosphorus in NPK mixtures and helps in the formation of carbohydrates in the plant. It also assists cambium development which causes the increased girth of plant limbs and stalks. A potassium deficiency causes strangely shaped fruits and foliage blotching.

Calcium, magnesium and sulphur are needed in rather large quantities but are not often deficient in soils.

MINOR ELEMENTS The micronutrients boron, iron, zinc, copper, manganese, molybdenum and chlorine are used in small amounts and aren't as often deficient in soils as some of the major elements.

Complete garden fertilisers containing different percentages of the major elements NPK and trace elements are available from garden suppliers. A particular crop may respond better to one mixture than to another according to the type of crop and age — seeds and seedlings or mature plants and — the pH of the soil.

To apply dry or granular complete fertilisers the banding method is safest. Having prepared a rather wide row for seedlings or seeds, place fertiliser in two narrow strips along the base of the row, and to the side, not directly under the roots. Cover the fertiliser with some soil and then plant out the seeds or seedlings. This method allows the plants to seek out the fertiliser when required during growth.

Water-soluble complete fertilisers such as Aquasol, Thrive and Zest can be used in diluted solutions and are useful as 'booster' fertilisers for food-crops.

PH TESTING

Testing the soil for pH is a method of obtaining a chemical reaction to determine the degree of acidity or alkalinity of the soil. It is measured on a scale from 0 to 14; pH 7.0 is neutral, above pH 7.0 is alkaline and below pH 7.0 is acid.

The availability of macro and micro nutrients for plants is affected by pH. In highly acidic soils there is a marked drop in the availability of the macro nutrients (nitrogen, phosphorus, potassium, sulphur, calcium and magnesium). In alkaline soils the micro nutrients (trace elements) become unavailable, and in highly alkaline soil some can become toxic.

Increases up and down the pH scale are tenfold per unit, thus pH 5.0 is ten times more acid than pH 6.0. The most suitable pH for vegetable growing is pH 6.5 tending to slight acidity, and can be achieved with either sandy or clay soils. A gardener can build up the soil to obtain the required pH level by adding mineral amendments until the measure is obtained, in order to produce high quality food crops.

Correcting an acidic condition requires the application of lime. At the other end of the scale, excess alkalinity may be corrected by sulphur dressing using flowers of sulphur. Alternatively, adding organic matter will form acids which will lower the soil's pH. Leafmould, pine needles and peat moss are especially effective.

A gardener may carry out a simple pH test using one of several pH kits available from garden and nursery suppliers.

ADDING LIME

Where the acidity of soil must be reduced to grow food crops, give the soil a lime dressing. Lime contains calcium, which in itself is not a major plant food, but it brings about a less acidic, more-alkaline soil reaction, which encourages bacterial proliferation and in turn leads to chemical changes in other soil minerals making them available as plant foods.

Fertilising acidic soil without pre-liming may be a waste of time and materials, soon evident by a lack of plant response. Nevertheless, a gardener should not apply lime on the assumption that it is needed. A pH test will indicate the need for lime. Lime is persistently leached from the soil, so high rainfall areas are usually in more need of liming than are drier areas.

Use agricultural lime (calcium carbonate) or dolomite which includes magnesium as well as calcium. A general lime application with agricultural lime should be 200 g per

PLANT NUTRIENTS
PLANTS' RESPONSE TO DIFFERENT COMBINATIONS OF ESSENTIAL PLANT FOODS.

square metre on acidic coastal soils and 400 g per square metre on clay soils, to be repeated annually. Garden soil is usually limed in autumn, followed after a suitable interval by fertilising if necessary. Where rainfall is heavy, however, it may be necessary to lime in spring and autumn.

Watering and Moisture Conservation

Fruit and vegetables need regular watering during their growing period. Easy access to water in the food-crop garden is essential. A permanent fixture for a simple irrigation system is ideal but expensive to install, so at least make provision for a tap to be close by for attachment of a hose or use of a watering can.

Lack of water or periods of moisture stress cause stunted growth and low yields of fruit and vegetables. Leaf, stem, and root crops become tough and stringy. Splits and cracks develop in carrots and other root crops. Fruit and seed vegetables become dry and shrivelled.

The quantity of water and the frequency of watering will depend on the water-holding capacity of the soil: clay soils hold water well, sandy soils hold water poorly. The time of year and weather conditions also influence watering, as does the root depth of different vegetables. Those with shallow roots (cabbage, spinach, lettuce, onion, sweet corn) require more frequent watering than deep-rooted vegetables. Also, vegetables use and transpire more water as they become larger and their leaf area greater. For example, a fully grown tomato plant bearing a heavy crop of fruit may require 20–30 litres of water on one summer day.

Despite the type of vegetable, its developmental stage or the structure of the soil supporting it, all species use water most efficiently when the soil is at or near field capacity. Field capacity describes soil that has been thoroughly drenched then surplus water drained away.

Sandy soils have a much lower field capacity than loam or clay soils. In summer, vegetables grown on sandy soil may need daily watering but those on heavier soils can usually get by with a watering once or perhaps twice each week. Whatever the soil structure, always give a thorough soaking to bring the soil to field capacity and encourage deep roots. A light sprinkle will not replenish moisture in the root zone and the surface soil soon dries out.

Never wait until vegetables start wilting before watering for they do not take kindly to this 'on-and-off' treatment. If the soil is dry just below the surface, then it is time to water. Vegetables with large leaves like cabbage, lettuce and cucurbits often wilt on very hot days when they lose water faster than their roots can take it up. The plants recover from this temporary shortage in the cool of the evening. However, another watering next morning will help the plants to recover and replenish the moisture lost. Water early morning or evening to avoid high evaporation in the middle of the day. In hot, summer weather, an early-morning, overhead watering helps pollination and seed setting in beans, sweet corn, and to a lesser extent in capsicum, tomato and eggplant. During cold, winter months, loss of moisture by evaporation from soil or from leaves is dramatically reduced. Winter vegetables often receive too much water so again apply the test. If the soil is dry just below the surface, another watering is required.

WATERING METHODS

Drip irrigation efficiently utilises the water applied, which is very important in conserving this scarce resource. With this method, water contacts the soil without disturbing the soil structure, the flow is controlled, the supply is uniform and constant and high water pressure is not required. A system is readily constructed using commercially available perforated black hosing. Small holes are punctured in the hose at intervals and buried next to the plants. Valves control the rate of water flow for individual crops and can be adjusted for local evaporative conditions.

Overhead sprinklers are convenient for the vegetable garden but choose ones with a fine spray because large water droplets will pack the soil surface. A fine spray also has a low application rate which gives better soil penetration and less run-off on sloping sites.

A garden hose with adjustable nozzle for spray width and droplet size may be old fashioned but it is still effective for watering whole beds or sections of beds. A water-breaker nozzle is an excellent hose attachment for watering seeds, seedlings and small plants. This nozzle gives a full volume of water in a soft spray.

Furrow irrigation is a useful method of watering on flat sites or those with a gentle slope. Make furrows with a slight fall to one end between rows with the edge of a hoe, building up the soil around the base of the plants (hilling) at the same time. Fill the furrow with water from a slow-running hose. Beans, potatoes, tomatoes and sweet corn are healthier when watered this way.

Mulching conserves soil moisture, particularly in summer when evaporation is high. A mulch also maintains a more even soil temperature and discourages weeds. Compost, leaf-mould, well rotted manure or dry grass clippings are recommended. Scatter 2–3 cm deep around individual plants or between rows during the warmer months. These mulches will rot down and can be incorporated in the soil when preparing for the next crop. Black polythene can be used for mulching beds containing potatoes, tomatoes or strawberries. It makes an efficient mulch and increases the temperature of the soil, so it is useful for early spring plantings.

Mulching vegetable beds in winter is rarely advisable, for by keeping the soil damp and cold a mulch may do more harm than good.

PERMANENT SPRINKLER SYSTEMS PROVIDE FOR EASE OF WATERING IN THE VEGETABLE PLOT.

Propagation From Seed

For seeds to germinate and grow, viable seed, air, moisture and suitable temperature are required. Seeds can either be sown in punnets or trays and later transplanted to the vegetable garden or sown directly.

SOWING IN PUNNETS

A reliable seed-growing medium can be mixed from equal parts of sand, peat or vermiculite. This will make an almost sterile, loose but moisture-retaining medium into which the seed will send its delicate roots. Fill the punnet or tray with the mixture and firm down, leaving 2 cm below the rim to allow for watering. Sprinkle seed over; mixing the seed with sand allows for even distribution of fine seed. Use a wire sieve to drift fine soil over the seeds. The depth over the seed should be approximately twice the diameter of the seed. Firm the soil down over the seeds by pressing with a level piece of board. Water and keep in a moist condition. When sown in punnets infant plants can be shielded against burning sun or wind by covering with paper or hessian and later hardened by gradually removing the covering.

When young plants growing in punnets have developed their first true set of leaves, after the cotyledons or seed leaves, they can be pricked out and transplanted to a permanent position. In spring, never put out seedlings before the last frost. Where night temperatures are low, transplants will take several weeks to start growing. Under normal conditions they should show growth eight to ten days after transplanting to a permanent position.

SOWING DIRECT

Large vegetable seeds or seeds of species that don't take kindly to transplanting are sown on the site in drills. Prepare the soil by working to a fine tilth. Mark the drills by impressing the soil with the edge of a board made for that purpose or use the handle of a garden rake. This will make a furrow at the same time as it compresses the soil. If fertiliser is added at the same time it must be placed in the bottom of the furrow in a fine drizzle and covered with 2 cm of soil before the seeds are planted. This practice is also necessary when seedlings are being planted out, and the depth of the furrow must be increased accordingly.

Sow seeds at required spacings. Small seeds can be mixed with sand for even distribution. Keep seeds well watered; never allow seed drills to dry out. The developing plant is at its most vulnerable when it is sending out its first roots, followed by the first two leaves. Keep the soil damp but not wet, warm but never hot. In a garden situation plants emerging in seed drills tolerate much more light and warmth than seedlings in punnets but must always be kept moist.

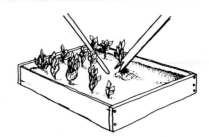

When the first pair of true leaves has developed (the first leaves to emerge are the seed leaves), transplant seedlings into the garden.

With a plentiful strike, be ruthless in thinning out the seedling plants. Do it while they are small so that neighbouring plants are not interfered with. Plants need adequate living space: highly intensive food cropping l eads inevitably to a lower harvest per plant and soil impoverishment.

Food-crops in Containers

Raise vegetable crops or fruit plants in containers, and a well-cared-for specimen in a suitable pot can enhance a patio or sunroom no less than a hothouse orchid. On the practical side, the mobility and protection afforded these plants is considerable, for they may be placed out of chilling or drying winds or given longer light hours by being moved from a morning to an afternoon position. They can be kept warmer and brought inside when frosts threaten. Growing vegetables in containers offers positive control over the soil mixture, moisture and nutrients. They are also more easily observed during all stages of growth.

Growing vegetables in containers has a special appeal for people who live in flats, home units and town houses. Tubs, pots and troughs offer a simple way of providing every home

Seed Sowing Hints

Prepare a seed-raising soil mixture.
Use reliable seed.
Never let the soil dry out.
Shelter from too much sun and wind.
Thin out as necessary.

Planting Guide

VEGETABLE/FRUIT	APPROXIMATE SPACE BETWEEN PLANTS	APPROXIMATE SPACE BETWEEN ROWS	DEPTH OF SEED	PROPAGATION METHOD
Artichoke, globe	100–125 cm	90 cm		Suckers
Asparagus	60 cm	60 cm	2–3 cm	Crowns/seed
Beans, broad	15 cm	60–70 cm	4–5 cm	Seed direct
Beans, French (dwarf)	10 cm	45–60 cm	2–3 cm	Seed direct
Beans, climbing	10–15 cm	70–75 cm	2–3 cm	Seed direct
Beans, scarlet runner	15–25 cm	70–75 cm	2–3 cm	Seed direct
Beetroot	10 cm	20–30 cm	1.2 cm	Seed direct
Bitter gourd	50 cm	50 cm	2 cm	Seed direct
Bok Choy	20–30 cm	20–30 cm	1 cm	Seed direct
Broccoli	50 cm	50 cm	1 cm	Seed or seedlings
Brussels sprouts	60 cm	60 cm	1 cm	Seed or seedlings
Cabbage	45–60 cm	70 cm	1 cm	Seed or seedlings
Cape gooseberry	100 cm	100 cm	1 cm	Seed
Capsicum	45–60 cm	60–90 cm	1 cm	Seed or seedlings
Carrot	5 cm	20–30 cm	0.5 cm	Seed direct
Cauliflower	50–70 cm	60–90 cm	1 cm	Seed or seedlings
Celery	20–25 cm	60–65 cm	0.5 cm	Seed or seedlings
Chinese cabbage	40 cm	40 cm	1 cm	Seed direct
Chives	20–25 cm	30 cm	0.5 cm	Seed or division
Choko	60–70 cm		5 cm	Fruit
Corn	25–30 cm	25–30 cm	2.5–3 cm	Seed direct
Cucumber	100 cm	100 cm	2 cm	Seed or seedlings
Eggplant	45–60 cm	60–90 cm	0.5 cm	Seed or seedlings
Endive	20–30 cm	45–60 cm	0.25 cm	Seed direct
Garlic	7.5–15 cm	30–40 cm	8 cm	Cloves
Ginger	15–20 cm	15–20 cm	2–3 cm	Rhizomes
Gooseberry	80 cm	80 cm		Cuttings
Japanese bunching onion	3–6 cm	30 cm	0.5 cm	Sow direct or divide clumps
Japanese turnip	10–20 cm	45–55 cm	1 cm	Seed direct
Jerusalem artichoke	45 cm	100 cm	10–15 cm	Tubers
Kale	20–30 cm	45–60 cm	1 cm	Seed direct
Kohlrabi	20 cm	30 cm	0.5 cm	Seed or seedlings
Kiwi fruit				Seed (✳) or cuttings (▲)

■ – throughout season ● – early season ○ – late season ✱ – seed throughout season ▲ – cuttings in late season

PLANTING SEASON

TROPICAL				SUBTROPICAL				TEMPERATE				COLD			
SP.	S.	A.	W.	SP.	S.	A.	W.	SP.	S.	A.	W.	SP.	S.	A.	W.
■				■				●		■	■	■			○
						○	●				■				■
		■				■	●			■	●	■		●	
●	○	■	■	■	■	■	■	■	■			■	●		
●	○	■	■	■	■	■	■	■	●			■			
								■	●			■	●		
●	○	■	■	●	○	■	■	■	■	●		■	■	●	
■	■	■	■	■			■	■	●			○	●		
	○	■			○	■			○	■			○	■	
		■			○	■			○	■			■		
								■	●			■	■		
■		■	■	■	■	■	■	■	■	●		■	■	●	
■	■	■	■	■	■	■	○	■	●			■			
■	■	■	■	■	■	■	■	■	■			■	●		
■	●	■	■	■	■	■	■	■	■	●	○	■	■		
	○	●			○	●			■	●			■	●	
	○	●		○	■	●		■	■		○	■	●		
	○	■			○	●			○	■		■	■		
■	■	●		■	■	●		■	■	●		■	■	●	
■			○	■			○	■			○				
■	■	■	■	■	■		○	■	■			■	●		
■	■	■	■	■	■	●	○	■	●			○	■		
■	■	■	■	■	■	●		■				○			
		■	■			■	■	■	■			■	■		
			○				○				○	■			
●				●				●							
													●		
	○	■	●			■	●	■	■	■	■		○	■	
	○	■			○	■			○	●		■	■		○
■				■				■				■			
■		■	■	■	■	■	■	■	■	●		■	■	●	
	○	■			○	■			○	■			○		
				✱		▲		✱		▲					

Planting Guide

VEGETABLE/FRUIT	APPROXIMATE SPACE BETWEEN PLANTS	APPROXIMATE SPACE BETWEEN ROWS	DEPTH OF SEED	PROPAGATION METHOD
Leek	15–22 cm	30–45 cm	0.25 cm	Seed or seedlings
Lettuce	15–30 cm	30–45 cm	barely covered	Seed or seedlings
Luffa	50 cm	50 cm	2–3 cm	Seed direct
Marrow	100 cm	100 cm	2 cm	Seed or seedlings
Melon	100 cm	150 cm	2 cm	Seed direct
Okra	40 cm	50–90 cm	2 cm	Seed direct
Onion	5–7 cm	30–45 cm	2.5–5 cm	Seed or seedlings
Parsnip	8 cm	30 cm	1 cm	Seed direct
Passionfruit			5 cm	Seed
Peas	5 cm	45–60 cm	4–5 cm	Seed direct
Peas, snow	5 cm	45–60 cm	4–5 cm	Seed direct
Peas, sugar snap	5 cm	45–60 cm	4–5 cm	Seed direct
Potato	30–45 cm	80 cm	10–15 cm	Tubers
Pumpkin	100 cm	100 cm	2.5 cm	Seed direct
Radish	3–5 cm	15–20 cm	1 cm	Seed direct
Radish, long white	20 cm	60 cm	1 cm	Seed direct
Raspberry	75 cm	100 cm		Cuttings or suckers
Rhubarb	40–50 cm	40–50 cm	1 cm	Seed or crowns
Rosella	60 cm	100 cm	1 cm	Seed
Shallot	15–20 cm	30–45 cm	0.5 cm	Bulbs by division
Silver beet	30 cm	45–60 cm	2.5 cm	Seed or seedlings
Spinach	5–10 cm	30–60 cm	1 cm	Seed direct
Squash, summer	100 cm	100 cm	2 cm	Seed direct
Strawberry	20–30 cm	40 cm		Runners
Swede	7–10 cm	20–30 cm	1 cm	Seed direct
Sweet potato	45 cm	75 cm	5–7.5 cm	Tubers
Taro	70–100 cm	70–100 cm		Suckers
Tomato	45–90 cm	60–100 cm	1 cm	Seed or seedlings
Turnip	5–7.5 cm	30 cm	1 cm	Seed direct
Water chestnut	100 cm	100 cm	10 cm	Corms
Watermelon	100 cm	150–300 cm	2.5 cm	Seed direct
Zucchini	100 cm	100 cm	2 cm	Seed or seedlings

■ – throughout season   ● – early season   ○ – late season

PLANTING SEASON

TROPICAL				SUBTROPICAL				TEMPERATE				COLD			
SP.	S.	A.	W.	SP.	S.	A.	W.	SP.	S.	A.	W.	SP.	S.	A.	W.
		○	●		■	■		■	■	■		○	■		
■	■	■	■	■	■	■	■	■	■	■	■	■	■	■	■
■			○	■			○	■							
■	■	■	■	■	■		○	■	●			○	●		
■	■	■	■	■	■		■	■	●			○	●		
■	■	■	■	■	■		○	■	●			○	●		
	○	■			○	■			■	■				■	■
	■	■	●	○	■	■	■	■	■	●		■	■		
■	■	●		■	■	●		■	■	●					
	■	■				■	■		○	■	■	■			○
	■						■			■	■				○
	■						■			■	■				○
●		■	■	●		■	■	●	○		○	■	●		
■	■	■	■	■	■		○	■	●			○	●		
■	■	■	■	■	■	■	■	■	■	■	○	■	■	■	
■	■	■	■	■	■	■	■	■	■	■	○	■	■	■	
															■
	○	■		■	■	■		■	●		○	■	●		
●	■	■	■	■	●		○	■							
	○	■	●			■	●		○	■			○	■	
■	■	■	■	■	■	■	■	■	■	●	○	■	■		
		○	●			○	●		○	■	■		○	■	■
■	■	■	■	■	■		○	■	●			○	●		
		●				○		●		○		●		○	
	○	●			○	●			○	●		●	○		
■	■	●	○	■	■		○	■							
■	■	■	■	■											
■	■	■	■	■	■	■	■	■	●		○	○	●		
	○	■			○	■			○	●		■	■		○
■				■											
■	■	■	■	■	■		■	■	●			○	●		
■	■	■	■	■	■		○	■	●			○	●		

Organic Gardening

This method of gardening depends on using organic materials, or those derived from natural organisms which had life, instead of inorganic or chemical compounds and additives.

Organic gardening is very much a question of maintaining a healthy ecological balance. Its results are not only confined to the natural production of healthy plants, but can also increase the water retention of the soil and assist in the battle against soil erosion. Adding organic matter or compost will convey nitrogen and other elements to the soil; it will aerate and act as percolator to water entering the soil; improve soil structure, making it easier for roots to penetrate; and hold soluble nutrients available for the plant.

Once broken down, all the mineral elements in the compost are made available to another generation of plants. Through the decay of natural composts into the soil, all these benefits can be expected but the process may be slow. It will depend on the condition of the soil prior to the enrichment and also on the amount of compost added. The results usually justify the wait and the resulting cycle of naturally enriched soil provides better quality ornamental plants and edible crops.

The food-crop gardener can easily make compost from animal manures, leafmould, vegetable and fruit peelings, tea leaves, herbs and natural substances like seaweed. A compost heap can be planned or a special compost bin purchased or built; this just needs topping up and the compost allowed sufficient time to decay before being added to the soil. If well-made, it will have a loose structure, an inviting smell and be a rich chocolate colour.

It should be noted that if partially decomposed compost is added to soil, it is best done when the bed is lying fallow; otherwise it is necessary to add extra nitrogen to the soil to compensate for the absorption of soil nitrogen (which is therefore not available for plants) by the micro-organisms which break down the compost into humus.

Organic gardeners also rely on natural substances to minimise pests and diseases. For further information see pages 80 and 90–94.

with a supply of fresh vegetables. Relatively inexpensive lightweight containers, 'easy to apply' fertilisers and the development of early maturing, compact vegetable cultivars have made vegetable culture in containers a viable proposition.

Salad vegetables — capsicum, cucumber and lettuce — are popular for containers because of their high quality and flavour when freshly picked. A tomato or eggplant makes a handsome potted specimen when fruiting. Dwarf, compact cultivars of salad vegetables and others like bush squash and zucchini are ideal for pots. Small vegetables such as cress, mustard, radish and spring onions are also suited to pot culture. Try some of the baby vegetables which are currently popular such as beetroot, carrots, cabbage, cauliflower or cherry tomatoes, as they too are ideally suited to pots, tubs or troughs.

Vegetables which give a continuous harvest — silver beet, spinach, rhubarb and 'green' celery — are also recommended. A range of tall or climbing cultivars of beans, cucumbers and tomatoes can be trained on stakes or a trellis against a sunny wall. A potato planted in a nest of rotting straw above a deep pot of loamy soil will yield kilos of clean potatoes in the straw area while the roots penetrate down to feeding level.

There are so many options available that flat-dwellers or those with a small courtyard or patio need not think they

KITCHEN AND GARDEN WASTE CAN BE HYGENICALLY TURNED INTO FERTILE COMPOST, USING A COMPOST TUMBLER.

have to forego a food-crop garden when pots are an easy solution.

PRACTICAL REQUIREMENTS

Sunlight is an essential ingredient for success. The balcony or terrace housing your vegetable containers should have a sunny aspect for at least four hours each day. Containers can be moved as required to make the best use of light, warmth and shelter.

Drainage is excellent in container culture if a good quality potting mix is used. A wide range of commercially produced potting media is available, but avoid acidic types produced specifically for camellias and azaleas.

Plants like the soil about their roots to be warm in winter and cool in summer. Mulching around potted plants will help to keep the soil temperature stable as well as conserve moisture.

Container-grown vegetables cannot forage for moisture as garden vegetables do. In summer, vegetables may use several times their own weight in water every day so this calls for daily watering. Leave a space of 3–5 cm between the top of the soil and the rim of the container. Fill this space slowly with water until it weeps from the drainage holes. This restores the potting mix to field capacity (or as much as it can hold. See page 17).

Regular watering also results in loss of nutrients by leaching. These must be replenished by regular applications of fertiliser as the plants grow. For leafy vegetables, give side dressings of nitrogen fertiliser or liquid feeds of Aquasol, Thrive or Zest every week or two. For beans, capsicum, cucumber, marrow, pumpkin, squash and tomato, give side dressings of complete fertiliser (NPK 10:4:6) or liquid feeds every three weeks. An alternative method is to use one of the slow-release granular fertilisers such as Osmocote in addition to the pre-planting fertiliser (NPK 5:7:4) when preparing the soil mixture.

It is best to grow only one kind of vegetable in each container as different vegetables have varying cultural requirements. Always have several containers on hand so that successive plantings can be made while the previous crops are growing.

Containers

The most widely used tubs, pots or troughs are those made of plastic. They are relatively inexpensive, light to lift and easily cleaned for re-use. However, fruit and vegetables in containers can be ornamental as well as practical. Terracotta, ceramic or cement pots or wooden troughs are viable alternatives to the more basic containers. For larger vegetables — climbing beans, capsicum, cucumber, rhubarb, tomato and bush cultivars of marrow and squash — use tubs or large pots 25–50 cm in diameter and 25–40 cm deep. Pots 15 cm in diameter and depth are suitable for smaller vegetables and herbs. Troughs are usually about 20 cm wide, 15 cm deep and vary in length from 30–100 cm. They are suitable for carrots (stump-root cultivars), lettuce, radish, silver beet, spinach and spring onions.

VEGETABLES

There are many ways of categorising vegetables. They can be grouped together under families, or according to their temperature preference (cold or warm season), or by the commonality of their edible parts. In some species the fruit is eaten (tomato, cucumber); in others it is the root (carrots, radish), or the immature flower (cauliflower, broccoli). Here, all vegetables are listed according to their edible part: buds, bulbs, flowers, fruit, leaves, pods and seeds, roots, stems and tubers.

MANY VARIETIES OF HEALTHY FOOD-CROPS CAN BE RAISED IN THE HOME GARDEN.

Buds

Brussels Sprouts (*Brassica oleracea* var. *gemmifera*)

BRASSICACEAE FAMILY

Sprouts belong to the cabbage family and bear a crop of miniature cabbages clustered about the trunk and surrounded by loose crowns of cabbagy leaves. Brussels sprouts are biennial, requiring a cold period to flower. They are a useful vegetable for the autumn and winter and are best grown in a cool climate. Modern varieties tend to mature all their sprouts simultaneously. Older varieties start maturing at the bottom of the stem and develop upwards. To harvest, snap off the trunk as needed beginning near the ground when the first buds appear in the leaf axils. When sprouts are detached, their accompanying leaf must also be removed.

CULTIVATION Sprouts are tolerant of a wide range of soils, temperatures and treatment, although districts with cool to cold climates give best results. To obtain sweet, delicately flavoured sprouts, these slow-growing plants should not be checked by dryness or too much heat.

Sow seed in nursery beds or drills in October in cold climates; December to February in milder areas. Germinating temperature is 5–25°C. When the seedlings are carrying three or four leaves, transplant at 60 cm intervals into well-tilled beds which have been given a base dressing of complete fertiliser at the rate of 100 g per square metre. Rotted compost and animal manure incorporated into the soil beforehand should get the plants off to a good start. Apply water as needed and mulch around the plants to help conserve moisture and control weeds. If the plants are in a wind-exposed position either hill up the soil around the plant base or stake them. Make use of early- and late-maturing varieties to obtain an extended harvest.

VARIETIES 'Long Island Improved'; 'Ohiestone' (mid-season); 'Rasminda' (late season).

BRUSSELS SPROUTS IN FLOWER.

Growing Hints

Plant Sow seed or plant seedlings in late spring or early summer in cold districts; summer in mild, temperate areas.

Harvest 16–20 weeks after transplanting.

Fertilise Apply complete fertiliser dressing at a rate of ½ cup per square metre when preparing the bed, supported by side dressings of fertiliser to keep the plants from checking.

Planting for Average Family 10–15 plants in two successive crops.

Pests and Diseases Grey aphids, cabbage moth, cabbage white butterfly, blackleg, cutworms, black rot, downy mildew, ring spot, club root, damping off.

Bulbs

All bulb vegetables are of the family Amaryllidaceae. The main criterion for their successful growth is good soil drainage; if waterlogged the bulbs will rot.

Most bulb vegetables are perennial, the biennial onion being the exception. Propagation is mainly by division of clumps; onions are grown from seed.

The bulb section of the vegetable is the edible part, however with chives, leeks, Japanese bunching onion and shallots, the aerial shoots are eaten also.

No plant family is as important to cooking than that of the onion. It is a valued addition to a wide range of dishes and all good cooks know their onions.

For companion planting purposes, note that there is a mutual dislike between peas and beans and the Amaryllidaceae family, and therefore they should not be planted in close proximity.

Chives (*Allium schoenoprasum*)

AMARYLLIDACEAE FAMILY

Chives are considered to be a herb but can be easily accommodated in the vegetable garden. Perennial in habit, chives are small members of the onion family which develop into thick clumps of grassy leaves. Mild in flavour, they are useful as a garnish, in sauces, savouries and salads. Chives die down during winter but can be harvested for the rest of the year.

CULTIVATION Chives thrive in ordinary soils in sun or semi-shade. If left to their own devices at the end of a garden bed or vegetable patch, they will happily produce abundant foliage.

Division of old clumps is the quickest method of propagation. Seed is slow to germinate but once past this stage it flourishes. Plant in clumps at 20 cm intervals in rows.

IVY HANSEN

BULB VEGETABLES INCLUDE ONIONS, GARLIC, LEEKS, SHALLOTS AND CHIVES.

Chives prefer a sandy soil with added organic matter. Good drainage is essential. A low nitrogen fertiliser should be incorporated into the bed at the preparation stage.

Chives are an excellent choice for pots and containers, and are great 'fillers' in the vegetable plot.

VARIETIES Common chives: *Allium schoenoprasum*. Garlic chives: *A. tuberosum* (Chinese plant providing good value for the small space it occupies).

Garlic
(*Allium sativum*)

AMARYLLIDACEAE FAMILY

Garlic is grown for its cloves which have a pungent flavour and odour, and are used in cooking for the flavouring of meats, dressings, bread, sauces and salads. The plant has an oval bulb with a membraneous cover enclosing a number of small, separate cloves. The leaves are long and narrow, and the flowers pinkish-white on long stems.

CULTIVATION As seeds are rarely produced, garlic must be propagated by the cloves planted in spring at a depth of 8 cm, spaced 15 cm apart within the row with 30–40 cm between the rows. Use only well-developed bulbs for propagation purposes.

Garlic can be easily grown in areas which are suitable for onions. It appreciates a rich, fertile loam but is otherwise undemanding except for occasional side dressings of a nitrogenous fertiliser and plenty of water during the growth period.

Plants are ready to harvest in about eight months after germination or when the top growth becomes dry and falls over in

---

Growing Hints

Plant Plant seed or divide clumps in spring, summer and early autumn.
Harvest As required as soon as leaves are long enough: from seed after 90 days; from division after 60 days.
Fertilise Liquid feed to boost leaf production.
Planting for Average Family Allow one to two clumps to develop.
Pests and Diseases Virtually free.

Growing Hints

Plant Plant cloves or bulblets in their permanent position in late winter in mild zones or in spring for cooler districts.
Harvest Approximately 8 months.
Fertilise Base feed with nitrogenous fertiliser.
Planting for Average Family 5–10 bulblets.
Pests and Diseases Thrips, downy mildew.

autumn. Pull the bulbs and sun-dry or leave to dry out in a cool, airy place. Braid the tops into ropes (see opposite) and hang up under cover or store in a net bag.

VARIETIES 'New Zealand Purple' has large cloves and a strong flavour. For small, flavoursome cloves choose from 'Italian Purple', 'Californian Late', 'Californian Early' and 'South Australian White'.

Japanese Bunching Onion (*Negi*) (*Allium fistulosum*)

AMARYLLIDACEAE FAMILY

Japanese bunching onion does not have a large bulb as such but is grown for its blanched thickened stem, 40–50 cm long. It is most popular in Asian cooking and is a close relative of the shallot. This species of onion is ideal for growing in a pot.

CULTIVATION Japanese bunching onions grow best in temperatures 15–20°C in deep, fertile, well-drained soil with alkaline to neutral pH. Apply lime at the bed-preparation stage if acidic soil predominates. Propagation is by division of existing clumps or sowing seed. Sow seed thickly then thin out if required, or start in a seedbed or punnet and transplant when 12 cm in height. Make rows 10 cm apart. Final spacing between plants should be 3–6 cm. Hill up around the stem during growth to blanch. Keep weeds under control by hand weeding or shallow cultivation.

VARIETIES Short bunching onion: summer type with short stems — 'Kyoto Market'; 'Asagi Bunching'. Long bunching onion: winter varieties with a single long stem — 'Ishikura'; 'Feast', 'Tsukuba'; 'Kiyotaki'.

Leek (*Allium ampeloprasum*)

AMARYLLIDACEAE FAMILY

Leeks are related to onions and garlic but are milder in flavour and do not form a bulb but rather produce a thick fleshy stalk. Culturally leeks are more adaptable than other members of the onion family. They are hardy enough to survive the severest of winters.

CULTIVATION Although fairly tolerant of a range of soils, leeks thrive in light, well-drained loam. As they dislike competition from weeds, sowing seeds in punnets and transplanting to a well- prepared bed is the most viable propagation method. Sow seed 1 cm deep and grow on until 15–20 cm tall. Transplant spacing seedlings 15 cm apart in rows at 20 cm intervals.

Bed preparation consists of digging a trench 15 cm deep and 10 cm wide and banding with a complete fertiliser at a rate of 5 g per metre along each side of the trench. Cover furrows with soil. Plant the seedlings along the furrows to a depth of 15 cm.

Water soil regularly. To harvest undercut leeks with a sharp knife when the stems are 20 mm in diameter.

VARIETIES 'Musselburgh'; 'Welsh Wonder'; 'Sleek' (available in punnets in spring).

Onion (*Allium cepa*)

AMARYLLIDACEAE FAMILY

Onions are biennial plants forming a bulb of thickened leaf scales on a disc-like stem in the first year, and a tall, flowering stem bearing a globe-shaped cluster of small greenish-white flowers in the second. They vary in bulb shape (oval, globe or flat), skin colour (white, yellow, brown or red) and flavour (mild, medium or pungent). Onions have a multitude of culinary uses. They can be eaten raw, pickled, boiled, fried and roasted, or used in soups, sauces, stews, curries and chutneys.

Growing Hints

Plant Year-round planting season; sow seed direct or divide clumps.
Harvest Short bunching onion 4–5 months; long bunching onion 8 months.
Fertilise Incorporate animal manure or organic matter dug in at bed-preparation stage.
Planting for Average Family Successive sewings of 1 m rows every 4–6 weeks.
Pests and Diseases Onion thrips, onion maggot, cutworms, weevils.

Growing Hints

Plant Sow seed or plant seedlings from early spring to autumn in temperate areas. In warmer areas sow late summer to autumn.
Harvest 16–20 weeks.
Fertilise Incorporate complete fertiliser at bed-preparation stage followed by liquid feeds every 2–3 weeks.
Planting for Average Family 40–50 plants.
Pests and Diseases Not serious.

Cultivars and Climate

Choosing the right cultivar and sowing the seed at the right time is vital for a successful onion crop. In sub tropical regions, early cultivars (sown late summer to late autumn) are suitable. In warm temperate regions, sow early cultivars in autumn and mid-season cultivars in winter. In cold southern latitudes with short days in winter and long days in summer, sow early-, mid-season and late-maturing cultivars in succession from autumn through to early spring.

BRAID ONIONS PRIOR TO STORING.

CULTIVATION A light, well-drained medium to heavy loam with added organic matter in a sunny position is ideal for growing onions. Heavy or waterlogged soil is most unsuitable.

Prepare beds by incorporating organic matter; well-rotted animal manure is excellent. Onions do not tolerate acidity so pre-liming several weeks prior to planting is necessary in soils of low pH. In addition, broadcast two handfuls of complete fertiliser per square metre and fork over well. Aim to control weeds at the bed-preparation stage.

Onions can either be grown in seed boxes and transplanted, or sown directly into their permanent position then thinned out. Transplants and seeds are both shallow-sown. Make drills 5 cm deep and space seedlings 10 cm apart with 30 cm between rows. Tops of seedlings may be cut back to 2.5 cm and roots trimmed to leave 1–1.5 cm from the crown. When transplanting, be careful not to injure the necks of the young bulbs where disease may enter. Plant, cover with a sandy soil mixture, compost or vermiculite and firm down, ensuring they are not planted deeply. Bulb formation should be above or only slightly under the soil, so bulb rotting is avoided during rainy weather. If planting seed directly sow thickly and thin the seedlings, which usually emerge in 10 to 14 days, to 2–3 cm apart and later to 7–10 cm apart. Seedlings from the second thinning can be used as green or salad onions.

As the onion has a shallow root system, keep weeds at bay by hand weeding or shallow cultivation to ensure plants are not deprived of water and nutrients.

A complete fertiliser can be banded along each side of the row at planting time, however, should growth become static give light waterings of a foliar fertiliser. Growth is apparent in the increased girth of the bulbs and not in increased foliage.

Maturing times vary for different onions but it is usual for them to take six to eight months to develop. It is important to sow the appropriate variety for the season, otherwise expect poor crops. Maturity is indicated when the stems begin to yellow. Bend the stems backwards to expose the bulb to the sun. When tops have turned brown lift and spread out until they are shrivelled at the neck. Rub off outer skins and take off all but 15 cm of the dry neck tissue. Once the outside membrane has dried, braid the tops together (see below) and store in a cool, dry, well-ventilated place. Storing in onion bags is also appropriate. When packaging, watch for onions attempting regrowth or bolting to

---

Storing Onions

The best way to keep onions is to string them. To do this, leave the long, dry leaves on and take a metre length of thick string or thin twine. Loop the string over a hook and knot the ends. Weave the leaf of the first onion through the loop. Weave the leaves of the next onion tightly into the string and lay the onion on the first one. Continue letting the onions fall left and right. Hang in a cool, well ventilated, dry place.

ONION CULTIVARS

	MILD FLAVOUR	MEDIUM FLAVOUR	STRONG FLAVOUR
Early Season	'Early Barletta' 'Early Flat White' 'Calred Early'	'Hunter River White' 'Hunter River Brown' 'Gladallan Brown'	—
Mid-season	'Odourless'	'Red Italian'	'Creamgold' (lk)
Late Season	'Mild Red Odourless' 'White Spanish'(lk) 'Southport White Globe'	—	'Australian Brown' (lk)

(lk) long keeping — ideal for storage

seed; these plants should be rogued out for they will rot if placed in storage.

VARIETIES Many cultivars to suit a wide spectrum of climatic conditions are available.

Onions are sensitive to the number of light hours in the day. For the bulbs to form, the plants must be exposed to longer than a critical photoperiod. The length of this photoperiod depends on the variety. Unless the right variety is planted at the correct time bulbing may not occur.

Choose early, mid-season or late cultivars for specific regions. Early cultivars are 'short day' onions and late cultivars are 'long day' onions.

Growing Hints

Plant Sow seed or plant seedlings in autumn and winter in temperate areas.
Harvest 4 – 6 months from transplanting seedlings.
Fertilise Incorporate animal manure and/or organic matter dug into bed. Give light foliar feeds only if indicated.
Planting for Average Family
50 plants.
Pests and Diseases Onion thrips, downy mildew, white rot, neck rot.

Shallot (Eschalot) (*Allium cepa* var. *aggregatum*)

AMARYLLIDACEAE FAMILY

Shallots belong to the aggregatum group, which also includes the potato onion and the tree or Egyptian onion. They differ from the common onion by having bulbs which multiply freely, producing a large cluster of bulblets

which can be divided and replanted singly. Because of this very efficient method of vegetative reproduction, shallots and other aggregatum onions are perennial and are propagated by bulbs rather than seeds.

The common shallot has an elongated, pear-shaped bulb. The 'Jersey' shallot has more compressed bulbs sometimes larger in diameter than in length. Shallots have a milder, more delicate flavour than onions.

CULTIVATION Shallots need a friable, well-drained, fertile soil which has been enriched with organic matter and a pre-planting fertiliser (NPK 5:7:4). Mother bulbs should be planted 15–20 cm apart. As daughter bulbs develop, hill the soil around the plants to blanch the stems. Side dress monthly with a high-nitrogen water-soluble fertiliser to encourage the quick growth of bulbs and stems.

Plants can be harvested as chopped leaves (like chives), as green onions (bulbs and blanched stems) for salads, as dry bulbs for flavouring (like garlic) or for pickling. Pull the stems when they are about 6 mm in diameter. Small daughter bulblets can be replanted for the next crop. Select bulblets from productive plants and ensure they are sound and unblemished before replanting.

VARIETIES 'Jersey'; 'Shallot Salad Onions'.

Growing Hints

Plant Plant bulbs from division of clump.
Harvest 8 – 12 weeks.
Fertilise As for onions but avoid using animal manure or blood and bone immediately before planting.
Planting for Average Family
Successive sowings of 1m rows.
Pests and Diseases Thrips, aphids, downy mildew, white rot.

Flowers

Vegetables cultivated for their edible flowers are the globe artichoke (family Asteraceae), cauliflower and broccoli (both brassicas).

The family Brassicaceae (mustard family) dominates the Asian vegetable scene. Cauliflower and broccoli are both cool-season vegetables; cauliflower being the more demanding of the two as it requires cool temperatures and short days to initiate curd development.

All the flower crops are heavy feeders and require well-prepared and fertilised beds plus side dressings during growth.

Artichoke, Globe (*Cynara scolymus*)

ASTERACEAE FAMILY

Artichokes are perennial and require a permanent bed. They grow 1.5 m high and their attractive radiating foliage resembles the thistle to which they are related. The artichoke yields very little for the garden space it occupies, but an odd corner in the garden may be found where it can be left undisturbed for three to four years. The solid centre of the flower bud is the vegetable. Cut the big, bronzy buds with a short piece of stem attached while they are still firmly closed. Strip off the tough outer scales until the inner heart scales, paler and thicker at the base, are reached. These may be boiled or steamed. The flesh of very young buds may be eaten or in more developed buds the scales are sucked.

CULTIVATION Artichokes will grow in quite poor ground but large fleshy buds are produced only when the plant thrives in richly manured, well-fertilised, moist soil.

Seed sowing of artichokes is not recommended as quality varies. Use suckers taken off the parent plant. Replant these in late autumn or winter in frost-free climates and in late winter or spring in frosty

IVY HANSEN

BROCCOLI AND CAULIFLOWER ARE GROWN FOR THEIR EDIBLE FLOWERS.

areas. Space 1 m apart in wide rows and side dress with complete fertiliser as they approach budding. Nip out lateral buds to throw energy into central growth, for too many buds will reduce plant vigour.

In most cool to mild areas it is possible to have artichokes for Christmas. Cut the plant down in autumn and when regrowth starts in the spring, reduce the suckers to about four.

Growing Hints

Plant Plant suckers in late winter or spring.
Harvest Approximately 40 weeks.
Fertilise Apply a complete fertiliser in 1 or 2 side dressings.
Planting for Average Family 3 or 4 plants.
Pests and Diseases Aphids, crown rot. Pests and diseases are not usually a serious problem.

Replant with new suckers every three or four years for improved harvests.

VARIETIES 'Large Green'; 'Large Purple'.

Broccoli (*Brassica oleracea* var. *italica*)

BRASSICACEAE FAMILY

Broccoli is a cold-season vegetable. Apart from the common broccoli there are several types of asparagus broccoli (sprouting type) available in Asian shops, such as 'Fat Shan'. Seed may be hard to come by, however, specialty seed clubs and heritage seed stockists are an excellent starting point for obtaining many unusual vegetable varieties.

CULTIVATION Broccoli is an accommodating vegetable which grows on light to heavy soils if sufficient fertiliser has been provided. Grow it fast to keep the tissues tender. Plants whose growth is checked are poorer in quality than those grown quickly. Best results are obtained by planting the crop in soil which has recently

grown legumes. Side dressing with a highly nitrogenous fertiliser boosts the plants.

Raise seedlings throughout late summer. Use a protected area at the end of a garden bed where the soil has been worked down to a fine tilth and lightly dusted with superphosphate. Firm the soil with a piece of board and sprinkle seed thinly. Cover with fine sand. Firm the surface and never let the seedbed dry out during germination.

When seedlings have four leaves, cut away one-third of the foliage. Lift the plants leaving soil about the roots and plant in rows at 50 cm intervals in a bed prepared with a heavy dressing of fertiliser at the rate of 100 g per square metre. Shelter the plants for several days until they begin growing.

Broccoli needs ample and regular watering to maintain satisfactory growth.

The large central head of densely packed flower buds, measuring 15–20 cm across, should be harvested before the buds open and show their typical yellow colouration. Smaller side buds appear lower down the plant; they never achieve the size or height of the first head but can be of excellent quality. Begin a continuous harvest over several weeks in cool weather.

Sometimes small leaves thrust up between the buds. These should be removed before they begin to absorb energy to the detriment of the flower buds. Where the bud clusters are of open, loose character the cause is almost certainly excess fertiliser.

VARIETIES 'Green Sprouting' — bluish-green smallish heads; 'Five Star Premium' — large heads of excellent flavour, heat tolerant; 'Romanesco' — light green colour, delicate flavour; 'Green Dragon Hybrid' — available in punnets in spring.

Cauliflower (*Brassica oleracea* var. *botrytis*)

BRASSICACEAE FAMILY

Although a herbaceous biennial, cauliflower is treated in garden cultivation as an annual. The plants have a single, short stem with large, erect or in-folding leaves. The stem terminates in a swollen flower head consisting of a tightly packed mass of undeveloped white or creamy white buds (the curd). A few varieties have purple curds which turn green on cooking. If the curds are not harvested, they break open to produce flowering stems and seeds in the second year.

A number of different varieties are available to be planted in summer and mature in the cooler months, then cut during the autumn, winter or spring, depending on whether a long-, medium- or short-maturing variety is chosen.

CULTIVATION Cauliflower is a cool season vegetable and is more demanding in its climatic requirements than the other members of the *Brassica* family. Cauliflower is difficult to grow in warm regions because a cold temperature is necessary to initiate flower (curd) development. In temperate and cool climates, sow seed in mid- to late summer to ensure plants develop a decent frame of leaves before the cooler autumn and winter months. By selecting from each of the three variety groups — early, mid-season and late — it is possible to harvest cauliflowers over an extended period of 10 to 12 weeks.

Cauliflowers thrive in a sunny position in a deeply dug, well manured loam. Good drainage is essential. Prepare the bed three

---

Growing Hints

Plant Sow seed or plant seedlings in summer. Germinating temperature is 5–25°C.
Harvest 16 weeks from seed, 12 weeks from seedlings.
Fertilise Apply nitrogenous side dressings or foliar feeds.
Planting for Average Family 10–15 plants.
Pests and Diseases Cabbage white butterfly, cabbage moth, aphids, whiptail, downy mildew.

'Mini' Cauliflowers

'Mini' cauliflowers are easy to grow and can be spaced at close intervals to produce a crop of small 10 cm curds. They mature in only 4 months from sowing. Seed is available from seed clubs.

CAULIFLOWER VARIETIES

	CULTIVAR	WEEKS TO HARVEST	FURTHER INFORMATION
Early Varieties	'Phenomenal Early'	6–16	Best early variety. Seed.
	'Snowball Early'	12	Cold climates only. Seed.
	'Early Purple Head'	12	Seed.
	'South Australian Early'	14	Seedlings.
	'Snowcrown'	9–10	Medium-sized, dome-shaped curd.
Mid-season Varieties	'Deepheart'	20	Best mid-season variety, large curd.
	'White Knight'	17–18	Large solid heads, firm white curd.
	'Hawkesbury Solid White'	18	Seed.
	'Snowmarch'	20	Domed, firm white curd. Dry areas.
Late Varieties	'Paleface'	24	Adaptable. Large curd, good colour.
	'Westralia'	24	Seedlings sometimes available.

TO PRESERVE A CAULIFLOWER'S WHITE, CRISP, CLEAN CURD, IT NEEDS PROTECTION. THE SIMPLEST WAY IS TO BREAK THE MIDRIBS OF THE LEAVES SO THAT THEY CAN BE BENT OVER TO COVER THE CURD. ALTERNATIVELY PULL SOME OF THE LARGER LEAVES IN OVER THE CURD AND FASTEN THEM WITH A TIE OF RAFFIA OR SOFT GARDEN TWINE.

weeks prior to setting out seedlings. In acidic soil, apply lime to raise the pH to 6.5–7.0. Add liberal amounts of animal manure or garden compost plus a pre-planting fertiliser at the rate of 100 g per square metre.

Germinate seeds in flats or punnets and prick out seedlings when large enough to handle into individual 10 cm pots to grow on until 15 cm tall. Transplant into a prepared bed, spacing the smaller varieties 50 cm apart and the larger ones at 60–70 cm intervals.

Cultivate between plants to destroy weeds and at the same time slightly hill the soil around each stem to give added support against strong winds. At no time should there be any set back to the growing plant from seedling to harvesting stage. To satisfy their fertiliser requirements apply side dressings of nitrogenous fertiliser or liquid feeds every two or three weeks during the growth period. Cauliflowers require a generous soaking of water once a week, making the roots move downwards in the soil.

Sometimes a nutritional deficiency of the trace element molybdenum causes whiptail and spoils the curd. Liming to reduce acidity releases this trace element, making it available to the plant. Alternatively, spray the plants once with sodium molybdate at the rate of 7 g in 11 litres of water as a preventative measure.

As the curds mature, tie their outer leaves over them to prevent discolouration and to keep them tender. To harvest, start cutting the curds early when they are tight and hard, before they open up. Quality deteriorates as they become soft and fuzzy. Early cutting will also spread the harvest.

VARIETIES Cauliflowers fall into three groups — early, mid-season and late maturers — taking varying numbers of weeks till harvest. Refer to the accompanying table to compare varieties.

Fruits

Vegetables grown for their fruits belong basically to two families. The family Solanaceae includes capsicum, eggplant and tomato and the family Cucurbitaceae is comprised of the vine crops. All fruit vegetables are warm-season plants which grow poorly at low temperatures and are frost-susceptible. Do not start them too early in spring before warm weather arrives. Planting in late summer must also be avoided because the crops will not have the time to reach maturity before autumn. In warm frost-free regions the growing period is not so critical.

Fruit crops can be grown in a soil that has been heavily manured before sowing. However, don't overdress with poultry manure as they need a higher ratio of phosphorus and potash compared to nitrogen. Nitrogen will promote too much leaf and reduce production of root and fruit.

Fruit vegetables bear flowers over an extended period so the fruits on individual plants are at different stages of maturity at the same time. In most cases fruits are harvested before fully mature and further ripening can be delayed by storing them at a low temperature. Regular picking of fruits will promote further flowering and better development of younger fruit. Melons, pumpkin and winter squash are exceptions; allow fruits to ripen on the vine before harvesting to develop full flavour and top eating quality. Pumpkin and winter squash are left on the

---

Growing Hints

Plant Sow seed or plant seedlings in warm ground, December to March. Germinating temperature 5–25°C.

Harvest 3–4 months after transplanting.

Fertilise Apply initial heavy dressing of fertiliser at rate of ½–1 cup per square metre and side dressings during growth period.

Planting for Average Family Plant 10–20 plants. Include several varieties to ensure successive cropping.

Pests and Diseases Cutworms, grey aphid, caterpillar of the white butterfly and cabbage moth, black rot, downy mildew, whiptail.

SUN-RIPENED, HOME-GROWN TOMATOES ARE FAR SUPERIOR IN QUALITY AND FLAVOUR TO COMMERCIALLY PRODUCED CROPS.

vine until it dies. This hardens the rind so that the fruits keep better in storage.

Many fruiting vegetables make attractive and productive container specimens. Tomatoes, eggplants, capsicums and chillies are all suitable.

Potted Capsicums

Capsicums are particularly ornamental plants and make attractive tub subjects for the patio, courtyard or sunny terrace. Water container-grown plants regularly and thoroughly as they dry out quickly causing loss of strength and blossom or fruit drop. Stout and sturdy plants, they need staking in windy positions. In frosty areas container-grown plants can be grown on over winter into the second season.

CAPSICUMS MAKE HANDSOME GARDEN PLANTS AS WELL AS PROVIDING PRODUCE FOR THE KITCHEN.

Capsicum
(Capsicum annuum)

SOLANACEAE FAMILY

Capsicums or peppers are many-branched shrubby plants, best treated as annuals although in warm climates they over-winter as biennials. The edible fruits differ greatly in size, shape and pungency.

Sweet peppers (bell peppers) have large, spherical, or tapering fruits with a mild taste. Eat raw in salads, hollow out and stuff with savoury mixtures for baking or cook in soup, stews or casseroles.

Hot peppers or chillies have smaller, pungent fruit which are used fresh or dried as paprika or cayenne, as a flavouring, for tabasco or chilli sauce and in curries or pickles.

CULTIVATION Capsicum is a warm-season crop requiring 14 to 16 weeks to mature from seed. In warm temperate frost-free regions, subtropical and tropical zones, capsicums can be sown and grown year round. In temperate climates sow seed from early spring to mid-summer. In cold climates sow in spring or early summer only.

The 1 m tall plants have a relatively deep root system and will adapt to most soils but require sharp drainage. Poor drainage combined with overwatering leads to damping off. The ideal growing medium is a fertile, well-manured, moist but well-drained soil with a pH of 7.0, which has been built up with compost. Occasional side dressings of complete fertiliser will boost the crop but highly nitrogenous ones are unsuitable.

Capsicum plants bear heavily so a few plants in the vegetable patch will suffice. Seeds can be sown in punnets and transplanted or sown direct, but in both cases the danger of frost must have passed when planted out in the field.

Prepare the bed well beforehand with moderate amounts of organic matter and rotted manure, and a pre-planting fertiliser (NPK 5:7:4) dug into the soil at the rate of 100 g per square metre.

If raising seeds in punnets, sow 10 mm deep in a friable mixture in late winter or early spring. Prick out the seedlings when large enough to handle into 10 cm pots and grow on in a sheltered sunny position. When seedlings are 15 cm tall and the soil temperature has increased, transfer them to the prepared bed. Space 45 cm apart within the row and 60 cm between rows. Capsicum

GERMINATING CHOKOS

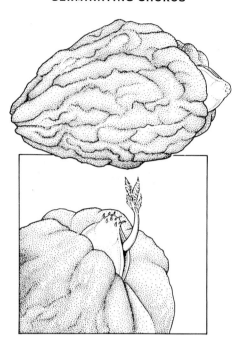

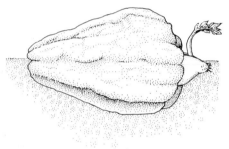

CHOKO SEEDS GERMINATE INSIDE THE FRUIT.
PLANT CHOKO AT SOIL LEVEL WHEN IT BEGINS TO SPROUT.

seeds may not germinate if soil temperature is too low. Gardeners wanting an early crop are advised to adopt this method.

Water well after transplanting. Do not force plants with additional fertiliser in the early stages. When flowering commences, scatter a complete fertiliser around each plant and repeat monthly while the plants are bearing. A mulch of dry grass clippings will prevent moisture evaporating and reduce weeds. Staking is only necessary in windy areas.

In most districts, capsicums grown from seedlings transplanted in spring will commence bearing around Christmas and continue to fruit until autumn. In warm climates consecutive sowings can be made every eight to ten weeks.

The fruits of sweet capsicums can be

picked at any stage of development. However, leaving the fruits of the 'Giant Bells' to mature will result in a sweeter flavour and development of striking yellow, orange and red colours. Hot capsicums have small, green tapered fruits in clusters. They are mature when they turn bright red.

VARIETIES 'Giant Bell' ('Californian Wonder') is the most widely grown sweet capsicum with large green fruit turning red. 'Yolo Wonder' is very similar. 'Gold Topaz' and 'Hungarian Yellow' produce fruit with golden yellow skin. 'Long Sweet Yellow' ('Sweet Banana') has tapered lime-green fruit, turning yellow with red or purple splashes. 'Sweet Mixed' contains both green and yellow fruits. 'Green Giant' and 'Sweet Mama' are available as seedlings in punnets in spring.

Growing Hints

Plant Sow seeds or transplant seedlings into warm spring ground.
Harvest 12 weeks from transplanting.
Fertilise Prepare bed initially with fertiliser and side dress with complete fertiliser.
Planting for Average Family 4 plants.
Pests and Diseases
Green vegetable bug, caterpillars, thrips, fruit fly, spotted wilt.

'Long Red Cayenne' is the best of the hot capsicums with small, green, tapered fruit turning bright red when mature. Other varieties include 'Red Chilli', 'Hot Chilli' and 'Tabasco'.

Seed clubs offer some interesting capsicum varieties in the 'Heirloom Series' covering all different shapes, sizes and colours. They include miniatures and chillies.

Choko
(*Sechium edule*)

CUCURBITACEAE FAMILY

Chokos are the fruit of a tendril climbing vine which can be planted in the home garden to cover out-of-the-way places like back fences or an old building.

The pear-shaped fruits are produced in abundance with skin colour varying from cream to green depending on the variety. The flesh is similar to that of summer squash in texture and flavour. Young fruit have the best quality for cooking and eating.

In hot tropical and warm humid zones the choko is perennial. In cooler regions treat it as an annual. The vine will crop in autumn and then later in the year it will bear a smaller crop, after which the vines should be cut back.

CULTIVATION Choko vines take up a lot of space and are ideally grown in an out-of-the-way part of the garden where they can run wild. They quickly cover any area where they can find support such as fence, trellis or shed. They prefer full sunlight but will tolerate partial shade.

Propagate the vine from a single choko — germination occurs inside the mature fruit. Select a smooth-skinned choko that is free from prickles and keep it indoors until the seed sprouts at the broad end and the shoot is 3–5 cm in length.

Prepare a planting hole 60–75 cm square by adding organic matter and a ration of pre-planting fertiliser (NPK 5:7:4) worked to a depth of 20 cm. Heap the soil from the sides of the plot to the centre to form a mound for drainage. Plant the choko in the centre of the mound with the top of the fruit at ground level with the shoot above.

Water amply in summer to maintain vigour and scatter side dressings of complete fertiliser high in nitrogen (NPK 10:4:6) around the plants two or three times during the growing season.

Pick the fruit when small for crisp texture and delicate flavour. Large chokos remaining on the vine for too long are coarsely textured and flavourless. Check the vines every three days for suitable harvests.

VARIETIES Propagate from high quality fruit (smooth skin, no prickles, mid-green skin colour).

Cucumber
(*Cucumis sativus*)

CUCURBITACEAE FAMILY

Cucumbers are succulent fruits of different sizes and shapes produced on an annual, herbaceous tendril vine. The edible fruit is a many-seeded berry containing a high percentage of water. The common cucumber is long and thin with a smooth green skin but other varieties are round or oval with skin colour varying from white through cream to green. The fruits of a few varieties have small, insignificant spines which are readily rubbed off, while others have prominent spines.

As it is a rampant spreader, the home gardener may have difficulty providing sufficient space for a cucumber crop. If space is at a premium, cucumbers can be grown on a fence or trellis to which the vines can be trained. Young vines may need some help by tying them to the support. Later tendrils will cling, eliminating the need for further tying. Growing cucumbers in this manner is not only an economy of space but provides a cleaner and healthier crop. Alternatively, consider the new bush cucumber 'Spacemaster' which takes up less space than the traditional vine.

CULTIVATION Cucumber is a warm-season vegetable and is frost-susceptible. In warm subtropical regions seed can be sown in almost any month of the year. In temperate climates sow seeds from spring to mid-summer. In colder climates with a short growing season make sowings from late spring to early summer only. Note that when sowing seed directly into the garden, the soil temperature should be 20°C or higher for successful germination.

Cucumbers prefer a well-drained, reasonably fertile soil which has been prepared with organic matter and a pre-planting fertiliser (NPK 5:7:4). If soil is acidic, sprinkle 200 g lime per square metre and dig over.

Traditional soil preparation entails forming 'nests' — raised saucer-shaped depressions which direct water to the plant roots. This mounding of the soil also ensures the roots remain cool on very hot days and provides quick drainage. Generous mulching affords the same protection to plants grown on flat beds.

Dust seed with a fungicide prior to sowing to reduce the chance of damping off. To sow direct, press five or six seeds in clumps to a depth of 2–3 cm in the hills which have been created 1 m apart. Do not overwater newly planted seeds — germination is best if kept on the dry side. After germination select the three sturdiest seedlings from each group and eliminate the rest.

To obtain early cucumbers or to grow cucumbers in areas where spring temperatures remain cool seeds can be started indoors in punnets, thus gaining four to six weeks on the growing season. Sow seeds in a friable potting mix. Prick out when the first true leaves have formed. Transfer to individual 10 cm pots to grow on in a sheltered, sunny spot until warm enough to plant out.

As the vines grow, the plants must have a plentiful supply of water. Their large leaves transpire equally large quantities of moisture. Mulching will reduce water loss and discourage weeds but keep the mulch 3–5 cm from the base

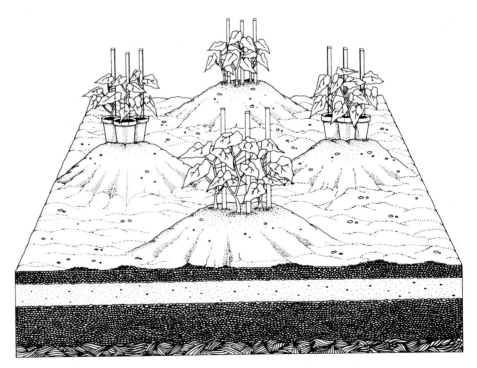

SET CUCUMBERS OUT ON HILLS 1–1.5 M APART, WITH SEVERAL PLANTS TO A HILL. AVOID ROOT DISTURBANCE WHEN PLANTING.

of the plants to prevent root rot. When flowering commences apply a complete fertiliser taking care to avoid leaf contact, or give liquid feeds of water-soluble fertiliser. Additional monthly side dressings or liquid feeds during the fruit-bearing stage are recommended. Nip off runners so that linear growth is aborted in favour of lateral stems, thence flowering and fruit setting.

Wind plays havoc with cucurbit vines. To prevent damage pin down leaders or train and tie the plant to a trellis.

Growing Hints

Plant Sow seed or plant seedlings in warm spring soil.
Harvest 8–12 weeks from seed.
Fertilise Apply liquid fertiliser for late varieties.
Planting for Average Family 3–5 plants.
Pests and Diseases Pumpkin beetle, 28-spotted ladybird, red spider, powdery mildew, downy mildew.

Cucumbers are monoecious, that is, bear separate male flowers (in clusters) and female flowers (solitary or in pairs) on the same plant. Crop failure can be attributed to poor pollination by bees, in which case hand pollination can help. Transfer the pollen from the anther of the male flower onto the stigma of the female flower using the same method as for pumpkins.

Most varieties will bear fruit eight to twelve weeks from seed sowing. When the vines begin fruiting, harvest regularly as the more fruit picked the heavier the yield. Harvest long green varieties when 5–10 cm for pickling as gherkins. When 15–20 cm long they are at their optimum for salad use. Apple cucumbers should

be picked when 10 cm in diameter.

If the fruit becomes too large, pick and discard it rather than leaving it on the vine to mature.

VARIETIES Slicing: 'Green Gem', 'Long Green Supermarket', 'Palmento' and 'Burpless Hybrid' — an excellent home garden variety with green thin-skinned fruit 25–30 cm long.

Pickling: 'Heinz Pickling', 'National Pickling', 'Pixie'. Apple: 'Crystal Apple', 'Richmond Green'. Lebanese: 'Mini Muncher' is a novel, small, smooth-skinned variety excellent for slicing or pickling.

Two cylindrical varieties — 'Patio Pik Hybrid' and 'Pot Luck Hybrid' — are suitable for growing in small gardens or in large pots or tubs.

'PATIO PIC' HYBRID IS SUITABLE FOR GROWING IN SMALL GARDENS OR IN LARGE POTS OR TUBS.

Eggplant (Aubergine) (*Solanum melongena*)

SOLANACEAE FAMILY

Eggplant is a member of the potato family and is grown in summer. As a relative of potatoes, tomatoes and capsicums, it should not be planted in soil previously used by these vegetables as it is prone to attack by the same soil-borne diseases. The handsome eggplant bushes grow to 90 cm in height and produce bright, purple-black globes protected by a prickly calyx.

Native to subtropical areas of Southeast Asia, eggplant requires warm conditions over a five-month growing period to give crops of good-quality fruit.

Eggplant makes a useful contribution to many national cuisines. It is used extensively in Asian cooking, and the small-sized eggplants used in Thai dishes are now readily available. To obtain seed for unusual varieties of common vegetables and also unusual vegetables such as tiny eggplants, consult catalogues of specialty vegetable seed companies, heritage seed suppliers and seed clubs.

Growing Hints

Plant Sow seed or transplant seedlings; germinating temperature 15–25°C.
Harvest 16 weeks from setting out.
Fertilise Add compost and generous amounts of animal manure at bed-preparation stage. Side dress with poultry manure when necessary.
Planting for Average Family 5–10 plants.
Pests and Diseases Spider mites, fruit fly, verticillium wilt.

CULTIVATION Eggplant is moderately deep-rooted and can be grown on a wide range of soils, the best being light textured, deep and free draining.

Seeds planted in peat pots and held indoors until spring temperatures reach 20°C can be planted out with safety at 60 cm intervals. The soil should be fair to rich after a previous crop. If the plants appear to be slowing up, side dressings of old poultry manure will give them a boost.

Harvest fruits by snipping with secateurs. Frequent harvesting will keep the plants bearing.

VARIETIES 'Yates Supreme' has large pear-shaped fruit and excellent flavour; 'Early Long Purple' is suitable for short-summer areas; 'Market Supreme' is available in punnets; and 'Black Bounty' from seed.

Marrow (*Cucurbita pepo*)

CUCURBITACEAE FAMILY

Marrows are warm-season crops, the fruits of which are harvested when immature and the skin or rind is still soft. They can be parboiled then stuffed with a savoury mixture of meat, onion and tomato for baking.

CULTIVATION In cold and temperate climates marrows should be sown in spring or early summer but in subtropical and tropical regions, seed can be sown year-round. Providing the soil temperature is

---

Pruning Marrow Vines

When two or three female flowers have set, nip off the growing tip of the runner to promote fruit development.

---

above 20°C, seeds can be sown directly into the garden. Early sowings can be made in pots and the seedlings grown on for transplanting in warm weather.

Soil must be well drained and prepared with organic matter and a pre-planting fertiliser (NPK 5:7:4). After dusting seeds with fungicide, sow three or four seeds in clumps or hills spaced 1 m apart. When seedlings emerge in seven to ten days, thin to the strongest seedling. If raising early seedlings in pots, transplant to the same distance.

In most districts, a spring sowing can be followed by a second sowing in early summer.

Water the plants regularly especially in hot weather. Scatter a mulch of dry grass

---

Spaghetti Squash

Buy a packet of spaghetti squash seeds and grow this marrow as a substitute for pasta. Simply boil the fruit and scoop out the long strands of flesh which resemble spaghetti. Each plant yields a half a dozen 20-cm marrows that have a shelf life of 2 months.

Growing Hints

Plant Sow seed in spring. Seedlings also available.
Harvest 10–12 weeks from sowing seed.
Fertilise Enrich bed with organic matter and complete fertiliser prior to sowing. Give side dressings of high-nitrogen fertiliser monthly subsequent to flowering.
Planting for Average Family 3–4 plants.
Pests and Diseases Powdery mildew, downy mildew, pumpkin beetle, 28-spotted ladybird.

---

clippings or well-rotted animal manure around each plant to conserve moisture and discourage weeds. When flowering starts, side dress with a complete or liquid fertiliser high in nitrogen (NPK 10:4:6). Repeat monthly while the plants are bearing.

Fruits of most cultivars are ready to pick in 10 to 12 weeks from sowing seed. Harvest regularly for quality fruit and to promote further flowering. To prevent damage to the plants, cut the fruit stalks with a sharp knife.

VARIETIES Both bush and vine types are available. Two recommended bush varieties are 'Long White Fruited Bush' with a white skin, and 'Long Green Fruited Bush' with a dark green skin.

Okra (*Abelmoschus esculentus*)

MALVACEAE FAMILY

Okra, or gumbo, grows to 2 m in height, with leaves 30 cm across and yellowish flowers with a red centre to 8 cm diameter. The cylindrical, green fruit grows to 20 cm long. This herbaceous annual is grown in the warmer areas of the world, mostly for the seed pods which are very nutritious; they can be dried for winter use and are used for thickening soups

---

Growing Hints

Plant Sow seed direct in spring, after the risk of frost has passed.
Harvest 14–16 weeks.
Fertilise Apply pre-planting complete fertiliser followed by side dressing of complete fertiliser mid-season or regular liquid feeds.
Planting for Average Family 6–8 plants
Pests and Diseases Not serious.

SCALLOPED SQUASH ARE AN EASY AND DELICIOUS VEGETABLE TO GROW.

and stews. The seeds also serve as a coffee substitute.

CULTIVATION The plant needs a reasonably fertile, well-drained soil, an open, sunny spot and ample water during dry periods. Repeated applications of liquid fertiliser encourage growth. As the plants do not transplant well, sow seeds direct after the soil has warmed up. Seeds are aversely sensitive to cold and wet soil. Sow 2–3 cm deep, spacing the plants 30–40 cm apart in rows for dwarf varieties and 45–90 cm apart for tall types. Pick the pods four to five days after the flowers have opened. Regular harvesting ensures continued good quality fruit.

VARIETIES 'Clemson Spineless'; 'Emerald'.

Pumpkin
(*Cucurbita maxima*)
CUCURBITACEAE FAMILY

The pumpkin is an annual plant with a long trailing vine. Like all *Cucurbita* species it is a warm-season crop and the fruit is harvested when fully mature.

Of the four different *Cucurbita* species — *C. pepo, C. moschata, C. maxima* and *C. mixta* — some cross-pollination is possible, which explains why there are such variations in size, shape and fruit colour.

Like other members of the cucurbit family, pumpkin plants have separate male flowers in clusters of two or three and solitary female flowers. After pollination the female flowers develop into a fruit with a hard tough skin surrounding yellow or orange flesh. Pumpkins can be boiled or baked, used in soups and chutneys and sweet or savoury baking. The flowers can be stuffed with a savoury mixture, dipped in batter and deep fried.

CULTIVATION Although pumpkin plants will tolerate partial shade they prefer a warm, sunny area with protection from strong winds. A long growing season of 16 to 20 weeks is needed depending on the cultivar. Generally they can be grown in all climatic zones except the very coldest.

Pumpkins thrive in soils that have been worked over with generous amounts of organic matter and are well drained but provided with adequate water.

Most pumpkin cultivars produce large, rambling vines and require ample space to grow. They may be allowed to scramble over a fence or garden shed. Ideally the vines can be trained onto a trellis, thereby reducing the chance of fungal disease entering through water splash.

In subtropical and tropical regions, sow seeds at any time of the year; in temperate and cold districts sow only in spring or early summer. As soon as the soil warms up after the danger of frost has passed, seeds can be sown directly into the soil. In regions with a short sowing season, early sowings can be made in punnets and the seedlings grown on for transplanting, allowing an extended period for development.

Prior to sowing, dust seeds with fungicide. Sow four to six seeds in raised

PUMPKIN VARIETIES

CULTIVAR	DESCRIPTION
'Baby Blue'	Roughly spherical shape with grey-blue skin and yellow to pale orange flesh on a compact, short vine. Early maturing — 14 weeks. Good storage life.
'Banana'	An elongated cylindrical shape with blue-grey soft skin. Long vine.
'Blue Max'	Bush type. Heavy yield of fruit with blue-grey rind like a smallish 'Queensland Blue'.
'Butter'	Cream rind, yellow flesh. Earlier to mature than other large varieties (14 weeks). Shelf life poor.
'Butterbush'	Small bush type, ideal for a small garden or large tub.
'Butternut'	Hearty cropper. Buff-brown pear-shaped fruit with orange flesh. Excellent storage life.
'Cinderella'	Bush type for a small garden.
'Crown Prince'	Drum-shaped fruit with thin creamy-grey skin and orange-red flesh. Takes 22 weeks to mature, with average storage life.
'Gamma' ('Trombone')	Long, curved horseshoe shape with orange skin and sweet, yellow flesh. Used mainly for jams and pies.
'Golden Nugget'	Small bush type taking up little room in a garden. Matures quickly, producing about 6 small orange-red pumpkins.
'Queensland Blue'	Large in size. An old favourite with a greenish-grey creased rind and deep orange flesh. Matures in 20 weeks. Stores well.
'Triamble'	Pale-grey, three-lobed triangular fruit with golden rather dry flesh. Tough skin. Yields well and keeps well.
'Windsor Black'	Large fruit. Dark green rind and orange flesh.

Pumpkins for Containers

Bush pumpkins such as 'Golden Nugget', 'Cinderella' and 'Butterbush' can be grown in large tubs.

'nests' as for cucumbers, 1 m apart; later thin to the three strongest seedlings. Do not overwater seeds immediately after sowing as keeping them on the dry side at this stage aids germination.

When plants are established, water regularly especially in hot weather. Watering cannot be overemphasised; the plants are highly prone to wilt in hot weather because moisture is lost quickly due to transpiration from the large leaves.

Mulching with dry grass clippings will conserve moisture and retard weed growth. As the vigorous vines quickly cover the soil between each hill, weeds seldom become a problem but any that do emerge need to be kept in check.

When the vines reach 1.5 – 2 m, tip prune to produce extra laterals and increase the number of female flowers. Apply a high-nitrogen (NPK 10:4:6) side dressing when flowering commences and repeat monthly while the plants are bearing. Avoid fertiliser contact with leaves. Liquid feeds of a soluble fertiliser are a suitable alternative.

Bees are the main pollinators of pumpkin flowers. Poor fruit setting can occur in cool, cloudy weather when bees are inactive but pollination usually improves with the return of bright, sunny days. Hand pollination is recommended if fruit set is not adequate. Pumpkin plants produce separate male and female flowers. Cut off the male flower early in the morning and remove the petals, then rub the pollen onto the stigma of the female flower just above the ovary. The female flower is identified by the small bulge at its base. When the ovary begins to expand both pollination and fertilisation have taken place.

The fruit of the pumpkin should be ripe 16 to 20 weeks after sowing. Never harvest pumpkins before the fruit is fully mature. Ripe fruit develops a richer flavour and stores better. Pick when the vines die and the fruit stalk turns brown and withers. When harvesting, always select fruit free of blemishes and broken rind as storage fungi can easily infect damaged tissues. When cutting, leave at least 8 cm of stalk attached to the fruit. This helps handling, improves storage life and prevents entry of disease organisms.

VARIETIES   Hundreds of pumpkin cultivars have been selected from natural crossings or developed by plant breeders. The accompanying table lists some of the most popular (see page 43).

Growing Hints

Plant Sow seed direct in spring; germinating temperature 12–35°C.
Harvest 16–20 weeks from seed.
Fertilise Incorporate manure and compost during bed preparation. Add complete fertiliser before sowing.
Planting for Average Family 2–3 plants.
Pests and Diseases Pumpkin beetle, 28-spotted ladybird, powdery mildew, downy mildew.

Summer Squash (Cucurbita pepo)

CUCURBITACEAE FAMILY

The term 'summer squash' is given to *Cucurbita* species with round fruits and scalloped edges, often referred to as 'pie-shaped' or 'patty-pan'.

The summer squash is a weak-stemmed, tender annual which grows as a bush rather than a vine. Separate male and female flowers are borne on the same plant.

Growing Hints

Plant Sow seed direct in spring.
Harvest 12–14 weeks from seed.
Fertilise Add organic matter and complete fertiliser at bed-preparation stage plus monthly side dressings of highly nitrogenous fertiliser after flowering.
Planting for Average Family 4–6 plants.
Pests and Diseases Powdery mildew, downy mildew, pumpkin beetle, 28-spotted ladybird.

The fruit is generally eaten in the immature stage before the skin hardens.

CULTIVATION   As for marrow.

VARIETIES   Scalloped fruit types include 'Early White Bush' and 'Early Golden Bush'.

Small bush cultivars of mini squash include 'Green Buttons Hybrid' (pale green skin), 'Scallopini Hybrid' (dark green skin) and 'Patty-Pan F1' (cream skin). Fruits of all three are best picked when 5–10 cm in diameter.

Tomato (Lycopersicon esculentum)

SOLANACEAE FAMILY

The tomato plant is a many-branched, summer-growing annual, bearing clusters of flowers which develop into fleshy, many-seeded fruits. Tomatoes are usually red and globe-shaped, sometimes with bulges or ridges, but some cultivars have egg-shaped or pear-shaped fruits or yellow skin and flesh.

The tomato is an excellent crop for the home garden because the plants give a high yield for the space occupied, and the fruit is picked over a period of two months.

Tomatoes for Containers

Tomatoes with cherry sized or mini fruit are ideal for pots and tubs. 'Small Fry Hybrid', 'Sweet Bite', 'Sweet 100 Hybrid', 'Tiny Tim' and 'Pixie Hybrid' all have cherry-sized fruit. 'Tigerella' has mini fruit with red and yellow flecks and stripes. 'Tommy Toe' also has mini-sized fruit, red in colour and delicious in flavour. Some are available in seed packs from general nursery outlets while others need to be ordered from seed clubs or seedsavers networks.

CULTIVATION Tomatoes are relatively demanding subjects requiring vigilant watering, pruning and fertilising in order to produce good yields. Despite this, they remain the most popular home-grown vegetable crop due to their luscious flavour compared to commercially produced counterparts.

Tomatoes are a year-round crop in frost-free subtropical regions. Two croppings are available in warm temperate gardens — in spring and early summer. In cold climates with a shorter growing season only one crop can be grown.

Good drainage is vital to tomato culture. The plants thrive in well-composted, richly manured soil with additions of complete fertiliser. Phosphorus is an important nutrient for tomatoes; lack of it in the early stages of growth can reduce fruit yield. Adding a pre-planting fertiliser (NPK 5:7:4) at the rate of 100 g per square metre ensures phosphorus is available. Add lime to neutralise very acidic soil.

Tomatoes may be raised either from seed (in situ if it is warm enough or in punnets if not) or be bought as seedlings.

If the soil and weather are sufficiently warm, sow several seeds directly into the soil in clumps and later thin to the strongest seedling. Ruthlessly roguing out all but the sturdiest plants is an important strategy for there are endless pests for the plants to fight and all but the healthiest will succumb.

To get plants off to an early spring start raise seedlings in containers. Sow about 25 seeds thinly in a tray of friable, well-drained seed-raising mix and place in a warm, shel-

Pruning Tomatoes

1 In each leaf joint a small bud develops. These should be nipped out.
2 Tomatoes grown without pruning axillary buds are said to be grown as 'bushes', often without staking. They bear heavy crops of smaller tomatoes, some of which will be spoiled by contact with the soil.
3 The flower and fruit clusters arise from the main stem between the leaf axils. When pruning out axillary buds, don't make the mistake of removing the flower buds. Pruned plants produce fewer fruits of much better quality and size. Often the weight of the fruit in total is as heavy as or greater than the weight gathered from 'bushes'.

TOMATO VARIETIES

Cultivar	Description
'Apollo'	Prolific, large-sized red fruit. Early-maturing. Needs staking and pruning. Cold-tolerant.
'Burnley Gem'	A main crop with round, medium-sized fruit. No staking or pruning required.
'First Prize'	Wilt-resistant. Available grafted.
'Grosse Lisse'	Popular globe-shaped red fruit. Mid-season variety. Staking and pruning necessary. Available grafted.
'Heirloom Beefsteak'	Heavy crop of large orange-yellow-red fruit. Juicy, flavoursome.
'Oxheart'	Large-sized fruit.
'Patio Hybrid'	A dwarf cultivar suited to pots and tubs. Medium-sized fruit. Plant needs staking and pruning.
'Red Cloud'	Orange-red fruit. Needs staking. Early-maturing.
'Red Peach'	Pinkish-red fruit. Dull fuzzy skin. Smallish size. Egg-shaped fruit. No staking required. Wilt-resistant.
'Roma'	Available grafted.
'Rouge de Marmande'	Medium-to-large ridged fruit. Compact grower. Early maturing. Cold-tolerant.
'Sweet Bite'	Cherry tomato. Easy to grow.
'Yellow Plum'	Egg-shaped yellow fruit. No staking or pruning required.

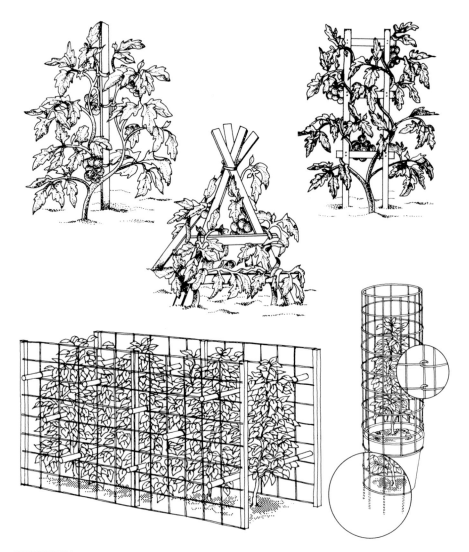

SUPPORTS FOR TOMATO PLANTS, USING MESH, MESH COLUMN, AND STAKES.

Growing Hints

Plant Sow seeds or plant seedlings as early in spring as the soil temperature permits.
Harvest 12–14 weeks after transplanting.
Fertilise Apply base dressing of complete fertiliser in heavily manured soil. Foliar spray at frequent intervals when fruit begins to set.
Planting for Average Family 10–12 plants.
Pests and Diseases Tomato mite, tomato caterpillar, fruit fly, aphids, nematodes, green vegetable bug, cutworms, bronze or spotted wilt, yellow wilt, fungal wilt, leaf spot, blossom end rot.

tered position. Seedlings will emerge in 10 to 14 days. Prick out into individual pots and grow on until 10–15 cm in height when they can be transplanted into the vegetable plot.

Plant spacing is important. For tall staking cultivars which are pruned to one or two leaders, plant 45–60 cm apart in rows at 1 m intervals. For non-staking cultivars, allow 75–100 cm between each plant. It is crucial that each plant goes into warm ground and is set at these intervals, as tomato plants are substantial feeders and require ample soil space to obtain their nutrients, and thus perform well and yield adequately.

Tall-growing tomato cultivars must be strongly supported with 2 m tall x 2.5 cm square stakes hammered into the soil 5 cm from each plant. Position the stake when planting seedlings. During the plant's growth tie leaders, making a figure of eight and allowing for stem expansion. When tying ensure that flower trusses are not squeezed between the leader and the stake. Carefully twist the trusses so that each flower faces outwards. In hot inland climates it is best to grow tomatoes on the ground with no pruning or staking because the vigorous canopy of leaves will protect the fruit from sun scald.

Correct pruning ensures successful cropping. As the plant gains height, prune the lower leaves which are touching or close to the soil. When 25 cm high prune to one or more leaders (main stems). Break off the lateral shoots in the leaf axils with a sideways action when immature or cut them with a sharp knife when larger. Finally, when the leaders reach the top of the stake cut the main shoot to prevent further growth, forcing plant energy into fruiting. Cultivars with large fruit are pruned to one or two leaders but those with cherry-sized fruit can be pruned to three or four. Also if trusses are limited to eight to ten per plant the size of the harvest will be increased in volume.

Providing a pre-planting fertiliser has been incorporated, additional feeding is not required until fruit set. When the first fruit truss appears, scatter 20–30 g complete fertiliser (NPK 10:4:6) around each plant and water in well. Repeat monthly during the fruit-bearing stage. It is important that this supplementary feeding be given in its most soluble and readily available form. Without supplementary fertilising, later trusses will ripen but the size of the fruit may be disappointing.

Cultivate between plants to destroy weeds. Mulch to suppress further weed growth and conserve moisture. Water the plants thoroughly once a week during initial growth but more often as the plants start to bear.

Fruit can be slow to set in cold snaps, on dull cloudy days or under windy conditions.

'GROSSE LISSE' IS THE MOST POPULAR MID-SEASON TOMATO. STAKE AND PRUNE TO PRODUCE A QUALITY CROP OF GLOBE-SHAPED, RED FRUIT.

BOTH THE FLOWERS AND FRUITS OF ZUCCHINI ARE EDIBLE.

Fertilisation will occur naturally when the temperature range is 15–22°C.

Tomatoes are best left to ripen to maturity on the bush. Slightly coloured fruit, however, will ripen well indoors.

VARIETIES Many hundreds of cultivars have been developed by cross-breeding. Heritage or rare seed clubs offer many interesting and unusual varieties for the connoisseur or gardener looking for a rarity. For a description of commonly available tomato cultivars consult the accompanying table (see page 45). Note that several grafted cultivars are available which are immune to virus diseases and produce a heavy yield.

Zucchini
(*Cucurbita pepo*)
CUCURBITACEAE FAMILY

A monoecious, herbaceous annual grown for its fruit which is picked when 10–20 cm long, the zucchini is a popular vegetable. As well as the fruit, the flowers can be eaten, either fried in batter or in salads. Bush varieties of zucchini such as 'Blackjack' are suitable for growing in containers 50–60 cm in diameter and 40–50 cm deep.

CULTIVATION Zucchinis require moderately rich soil supplemented with animal manures and copious, regular watering. They will grow unchecked through warm nights. The bush zucchinis are the fastest to make weight and their non-rambling habit has won them popularity.

Zucchinis are best harvested when 15 cm long. They should be picked frequently so that the vines will continue to bear. When plants go into a bearing phase, vegetative growth ceases while energy is expended on the fruit. If the fruit is not picked it continues to drain energy at the expense of producing more flowers. Yield is increased by constant harvesting.

Propagation is the same as for the marrow.

VARIETIES Recommended cultivars include 'Blackjack', a prolific bush type hybrid with a very dark green fruit; 'Greyzini', a high-yielding bush variety with greyish-green skin; and 'Goldzini' (yellow skin). Lebanese zucchinis which are lighter in skin colour, shorter and thicker are also deservedly popular.

> ## Growing Hints
>
> *Plant* Sow seed or plant seedlings in spring; germinating temperature 12–35°C.
> *Harvest* 7–8 weeks from transplanting seedlings.
> *Fertilise* Incorporate manure and compost during bed preparation. Add complete fertiliser before sowing seed or transplanting seedlings.
> *Planting for Average Family* 3–4 plants.
> *Pests and Diseases* Powdery mildew, downy mildew, pumpkin beetle, 28-spotted ladybird.

Leaf Crops

Leaf crops consist of vegetables of which the leaf is the edible part. They belong to a wide range of families including Asteraceae, Brassicaceae and Chenopodiaceae.

They are all cool to mid-season crops and must be grown quickly to produce best results.

In achieving maximum leaf growth they make heavy demands on nitrogen, and a well-prepared bed around neutral pH is necessary. Dig in heavy quantities of composted animal or poultry manure. Alternatively, use compost and supplement it with dressings of fertiliser rich in nitrogen. Don't use fertilisers rich in phosphorus or potash, as these have a tendency to make the plants run to seed. No lack of water can be allowed as any check in growth will tend to result in tough

LEAFY VEGETABLES — SILVER BEET, BOK CHOY, LETTUCE, ENDIVE, CABBAGE AND CHINESE CABBAGE — REQUIRE HEAVY DOSES OF NITROGENOUS FERTILISERS.

IVY HANSEN

Growing Hints

Plant Sow seed direct in late summer and autumn.
Harvest 8–10 weeks.
Fertilise Apply pre-planting fertiliser at rate of 100 g per square metre and nitrogenous side dressing fortnightly during growth.
Planting for Average Family 6–9 plants successively sown monthly.
Pests and Diseases Aphids, green looper caterpillar, bacterial soft rot, white rust.

leaves often quite bitter in flavour.

For all the leaf crops, sowing directly into the bed and thinning out is usually preferable to transplanting. The latter may check the plants' growth too severely and result in inferior quality.

All leafy vegetables have a short storage life once picked, so use them quickly.

Bok Choy
(*Brassica chinensis*)

BRASSICACEAE FAMILY

Bok choy is also called pak choy, spoon cabbage, mustard cabbage or Chinese chard. The plant does not form a head and resembles chard or silver beet in appearance. The broad, smooth-edged leaves taper to a narrow stalk 30 cm in length. The stalk may be white, yellow or lime-green according to variety. Bok Choy is widely used in Asian cooking.

CULTIVATION Bok choy is grown in much the same manner as ordinary cabbage, but it is less climatically adaptable. For best results, make sowings in late summer and autumn to grow through the cooler months.

Bok choy should be grown quickly. It requires ample water applied to a well-drained, fertile soil enriched with animal manure or compost and a ration of complete fertiliser (NPK 5:7:4). Add lime to very acidic soil. Asian vegetables tolerate slightly acidic soil: pH 6.0–7.0 ideal.

Always sow seed directly into soil as transplants are not suitable. Place a few seeds in clumps at 20–30 cm intervals. When seedlings emerge thin to the strongest plant.

Water well and mulch plants. A nitrogenous side dressing or water-soluble liquid fertiliser can be applied fortnightly.

Harvest bok choy as soon as it is mature (60–70 days), as it then begins to heart up. Cut the entire head off at ground level.

VARIETIES 'Pak Choy White'; 'Pak Choy Green'; 'Chinese Spinach'; 'Hypro F1'. All are non-heading varieties with spoon-shaped leaves and long stalks.

Cabbage (*Brassica oleracea* var. *capitata*)

BRASSICACEAE FAMILY

This biennial, leafy vegetable is popular and easy to grow. In garden cultivation it is treated as an annual. The condensed leaves fold inwards to form a dense 'head' which, when mature, can be chopped up and eaten raw as coleslaw, steamed or fermented to make sauerkraut.

Most varieties available are hybrids of different shapes and sizes that mature at different times. The three main types of cabbage are ballhead (roundhead), conical (sugarloaf), and the large drumhead type. The last is not suitable for the home garden. Savoy cabbages have wrinkled or blistered skin, while red cabbage is used mostly for pickling. Cabbages can also be classified as early, mid-season, and late winter varieties.

CULTIVATION Cabbages are more climatically adaptable than most *Brassicas*. Nevertheless, unsuccessful growth is due mainly to planting at the wrong time. In general, cabbages can be grown over a wide range of temperatures providing they are started in the warm weather and then mature in the cooler months. If sown in cold weather to mature in the warm season cabbages run to seed and the head loses its food value.

In subtropical areas sow year round. In tropical regions, sow seed any time of the year apart from the monsoonal season between December and March. In temperate and cold climates sow from early spring to autumn. Some varieties such as Savoy can stand slight frost when mature.

Cabbages must be grown quickly to form tight, solid heads. They prefer a sunny position in a light, moderately fertile, open loam through which the roots can forage easily. Well-rotted animal manure or garden

CABBAGES MUST BE GROWN QUICKLY TO FORM TIGHT, SOLID HEADS. APPLY SIDE DRESSINGS OF COMPLETE FERTILISER OR FOLIAR FEED WITH A LIQUID FERTILISER.

compost should be liberally added to the bed to ensure a degree of water-holding capacity. Drainage at root level must always be efficient.

At the bed-preparation stage add a complete fertiliser (NPK 5:7:4) at a rate of 100 g per square metre. If the soil is very acidic, add lime to bring pH to 6.0–6.5. Magnesium deficiency in the soil can be a problem with cabbage culture. Apply 0.5 kg of dolomite per square metre several weeks prior to seed sowing, if you are aware of such a deficiency. Magnesium deficiency shows up on the cabbages as yellowish areas between the veins and around the leaf margins of the older foliage together with a stunted appearance. If cabbages present these symptoms, water once with Epsom salts solution at a rate of 30 g in 5 litres of water.

Sow seeds in punnets, harden off and transplant when 10 cm high (about eight weeks). Alternatively sow a few seeds in a clump directly into the vegetable patch at a depth of 1.5 cm and thin to the strongest seedling. The distance between transplanted seedlings or clumps when sown direct depends on the variety of cabbage planted. Allow 40–50 cm intervals for small early-maturing varieties. Increase the distance to 60–70 cm for larger late-maturing varieties.

Small quantities of seed can be sown successively when the weather begins to warm up to keep cabbages in regular supply. Make subsequent sowings when seedlings from the previous plantings are 15–20 cm high.

During periods of active growth and especially in dry weather the plants require copious quantities of water at regular intervals. Cultivate between young plants to destroy weeds. Mulch to keep roots cool and prevent excessive moisture loss from the soil.

Cabbages are gross feeders, thriving in an enriched soil, preferably following a legume crop. They respond vigorously to fertilising providing the soil has been recently pre-limed. Liming also discounts the possibility of club root development, a common brassica problem. Club root can also be controlled by crop rotation. It is important to supplement feeding with inorganic fertilisers — scatter a nitrogenous fertiliser such as sulphate of ammonia around each plant at a rate of 30 g per square metre or give liquid feeds of water-soluble fertiliser every two to three weeks while the plants are growing. Regular feeding promotes rapid leaf growth and crisp, tight heads.

Different varieties of cabbage are ready to harvest at different times. Small early varieties are ready to harvest in eight to ten weeks from transplanting. Larger varieties include Savoy and red cabbage are ready in 12 to 16 weeks. Cabbages can be picked at any time after the heart begins to firm but it is preferable for the heart to become sound before cutting. A good test of this is when the head does not yield to pressure from the hands. If left too long the heads may split open.

VARIETIES Early maturing, round-headed varieties are 'Earliball', 'Velocity', 'Scarlet', 'Primo' and 'Supermarket'. Small conical varieties are 'Diadem', 'East Ham'

Growing Hints

Plant Sow seed or plant seedlings year-round in warm districts. Confine planting to July to March in cooler areas.
Harvest 12–16 weeks for seeds; 8–12 weeks for seedlings depending on variety.
Fertilise Apply complete fertiliser as base dressing and nitrogenous foliar feeds or side dressings.
Planting for Average Family 10–15 plants.
Pests and Diseases Grey aphids, white butterfly, cutworms, black beetle, cabbage moth, downy mildew, club root, blackleg, magnesium deficiency.

Seasonal Cropping

Broccoli

Cauliflower

Cabbage

Silver beet

It is important to keep the menu in mind when planting vegetables. Instead of a complete bed devoted to cabbages, plant one or two rows of the winter leafy vegetables and rotate with root vegetables for summer cropping.

and 'Enfield Market'. Early-maturing hybrids include 'Superette Hybrid' (round), 'Stonehead Hybrid' (round) and 'Sugarloaf Hybrid' (conical). Late-maturing varieties are 'Copenhagen Market', 'Large Sugarloaf', 'Oxheart' and 'Greengold Hybrid'. Savoys, with wrinkled leaves include 'Savoy Hybrid', 'Savoy King Hybrid' and 'Savoy Drumhead'. Red cabbage varieties are 'Red Hybrid', 'Red Pickling' and 'Mammoth Red Rock'.

Chinese Cabbage (Pe-tsai) (*Brassica pekinensis*)

BRASSICACEAE FAMILY

Chinese cabbages are natives of China and Japan where they have been used raw in salads or as cooked greens for thousands of years. They are more closely related to mustard than cabbage. There are two distinct forms — Bok choy (*Brassica chinensis*) and Pe-tsai (*B. pekinensis*).

Pe-tsai is similar in its growth to common cabbage, but the heads which may be densely packed or loose according to variety are narrow and more elongated. The leaves have prominent veins, toothed margins and are thinner than those of common cabbage.

CULTIVATION Chinese cabbage is grown in much the same way as common cabbage but is less adaptable to climatic variations. Seed sown in spring or early summer may produce plants which flower prematurely. Plants from seed sown in late summer or autumn are more reliable grown through the cooler months. Sow seeds directly into the garden because transplanted seedlings also tend to flower early.

Sow in clumps 40 cm apart each way and thin to the strongest seedling. Successive sowings can be made every three or four weeks.

Chinese cabbages must be grown quickly in a well-drained, fertile soil. Add liberal quantities of animal manure or garden compost and a ration of pre-planting fertiliser (NPK 5:7:4) when preparing the bed. Add lime if the soil is acidic. Keep plants well watered and spread a mulch of grass clippings or compost around them to keep the shallow roots cool and retard evaporation of moisture. Scatter a nitrogenous fertiliser at a rate of 30 g per square metre or give liquid feeds of one of the water-soluble fertilisers fortnightly.

Well-grown Chinese cabbages take eight to ten weeks from sowing to harvest. Pe-tsai types are ready to cut when the heads are squashy and yield to pressure.

VARIETIES 'Wong Bok' is the most common variety. Others include 'Chinese Hybrid', 'Pe-tsai', 'Michihli'.

Endive (*Cichorium endivia*)

ASTERACEAE FAMILY

Endive is a cool-season crop with narrow, finely cut, loose, fringed and curly leaves. It is a form of chicory and the leaves have a slightly bitter taste. It is hardier than lettuce and less prone to pests and diseases.

CULTIVATION Plant endives in rows 45–60 cm apart and at intervals of 20–30 cm. Shallow planting of seed is essential.

Endive responds to rich, well-composted soil, well-fertilised with a complete fertiliser and a uniform supply of water. Endive is frost-hardy and would be too bitter to enjoy were it not for the tenderising it receives while being blanched. Blanching is accomplished by upending a close-fitting box over each plant 20 to 30 days before picking. Alternatively, when the leaves are 25 cm long, gather together and tie them up so the heart becomes white (two to three weeks). Once the inner leaves have been blanched, they tend to be short-lived and must be used quickly.

To harvest, cut the entire head at its base. Discard the bitter outer leaves.

Bolting

The main problem in growing Chinese cabbage is bolting or premature flowering. Sow seeds directly into the garden rather than transplant seedlings. Grow the plants during the cooler months of the year and pay careful attention to watering and feeding to promote quick growth. Hybrids are less prone to bolting.

Growing Hints

Plant Sow seed direct in late summer and autumn.
Harvest 8–10 weeks from sowing.
Fertilise Apply pre-planting fertiliser at rate of 100 g per square metre and nitrogenous side dressing fortnightly during growth.
Planting for Average Family 6–9 plants successively sown every 4 weeks.
Pests and Diseases Aphids, green looper caterpillar, bacterial soft rot, white rust.

BLANCH ENDIVE TO REDUCE BITTERNESS IN THE LEAVES.

Growing Hints

Plant Sow seed direct in early spring for a summer crop and in late summer/early autumn for winter harvest.
Harvest 12–16 weeks.
Fertilise Create an enriched soil with a base dressing of complete fertiliser.
Planting for Average Family 10 plants.
Pests and Diseases Virtually free.

VARIETIES Winter type: 'Batavian Full Heart'; 'Broad Leaf Full Heart'. Summer type: 'Early Full Heart No. 5'; 'Green Curled'; 'Salad King'.

Kale
(*Brassica oleracea* var. *acephala*)

BRASSICACEAE FAMILY

'Curly kale' or 'curly cabbage' are common names for this handsome vegetable. It is a non-heading variety of cabbage with curly green leaves. It is very hardy and the flavour is improved by frost. More often admired for looks than for its palatableness, it can be harvested over a six month period on

Growing Hints

Plant Sow seed direct spring and summer.
Harvest Winter.
Fertilise As for cabbage.
Planting for Average Family 10 plants.
Pests and Diseases As for cabbage.

the cut-and-come-again principle by snapping off leaves as required. The plant can also be harvested whole by cutting at ground level.

CULTIVATION Its cultivation is the same as for cabbage in all respects.

VARIETIES 'Half-tall Scotch'; 'Georgia'; 'Ornamental'.

Lettuce
(*Lactuca sativa*)

ASTERACEAE FAMILY

The leaves of the lettuce plant are one of the most popular of salad vegetables, and in China lettuce is used for cooking and pickling. Although naturally a cool-weather plant lettuce cultivars have been developed to grow in warm weather and varieties are now available to suit all seasonal conditions. The four types of lettuce are head (crisphead or butterhead), looseleaf, cos or romanie, and stem.

CULTIVATION Lettuce plants can be grown in a wide range of moderately rich, well-drained soils. Both heavy and light soils are suitable, although light soils suit winter culture and heavy soils are best for summer growing. A pH of 6.0–6.5 is preferable. Lettuces are gross feeders and when provided with well-rotted poultry or cow manure dug in, the plants thrive.

Sow seed directly into finely tilled soil into drills 30 cm apart and cover with 1 cm of fine soil. Keep moist. When seedlings emerge, thin to 15–30 cm apart depending on the variety. Thinnings may be replanted to mature a little later.

Seeds may also be sown in punnets and transplanted when 5 cm high. Transplant on an overcast day if possible; seedlings of this size will suffer less setback if dull weather persists for several days after planting. Positioning at close intervals of 30 cm as recommended keeps soil temperature down in hot weather, thereby reducing evaporation. Mulching is also advisable.

Lettuces have poorly developed roots to support their massive leaf structure. Water is essential to maintain rapid growth as they are very prone to moisture stress. As with all

ornamental or food plants, water is best utilised when applied in the cool of the evening. Adequate moisture ensures that there is no check in the plants' growth which makes the leaves tough and bitter and causes bolting. The two commonest problems with lettuce culture are hindered seed germination because of soaring temperatures and existing crops bolting to seed.

With leaf crops such as lettuce any liquid fertiliser used to boost growth should be high in nitrogen.

Lettuce is a quick-growing crop so successive sowings of 5–10 seeds every fortnight through spring, summer and autumn, making best use of late maturing varieties, will give continual harvests. Butterhead and cos types are ready to harvest in 60–75 days. Pick crisphead types when the hearts are firm and crisp. They should not be left too long after this stage as they become bitter and slimy. Always harvest lettuce during the coolest part of the day — mornings or evenings.

VARIETIES Small varieties of lettuce are often preferred for the home garden. They also adapt well to pot culture as long as they are regularly watered. 'Mignonette' is a small variety which is particularly useful

Growing Hints

Plant Successive sowings in seedbeds or drills at any time except the hottest and coldest months of the year. Germinating temperature is 5–25°C.
Harvest 6–8 weeks after transplanting.
Fertilise Apply base fertilising of bed, together with rotted manures and compost. Give side dressing of nitrogenous fertiliser.
Planting for Average Family 5–10 plants every few weeks.
Pests and Diseases All leaf eaters, thrips, cutworms, aphids, necrotic yellow virus, downy mildew.

LETTUCE ARE GROSS FEEDERS AND THRIVE IN RICH, ORGANIC SOIL.

for hotter districts. 'Brown Red Mignonette' and 'Green Mignonette' are available in punnets. 'Cos' with its long leaves and 'Buttercrunch' with small, thick waxy leaves are also excellent home garden types. 'Red Oakleaf' and 'Lollo Rosso' (Coral Lettuce) may be available from specialty seed suppliers.

For larger lettuces suited to home growing, consider 'Great Lakes' which will not run to seed prematurely even in very hot weather. For plants maturing from late autumn to early spring choose from 'Winterlake' and 'Imperial Triumph'. For summer lettuce, plant 'Great Lakes', 'Pennlake', 'Imperial 847' and 'Yatesdale'.

Silver Beet (*Beta vulgaris* var. *cicla*)

CHENOPODIACEAE FAMILY

Silver beet or Swiss chard is often mistaken for spinach. However, silver beet is a different genus and has broad white leaf stalks while spinach has long green ones. Silver beet is most commonly grown in Australia. It is adaptable to both cool and warm climates.

It is one of the handiest pick-and-come-again of the leafy vegetables. Strong plants are prolific with leaf and, barring cold snaps which may send them prematurely bolting to seed, can be picked over several months. Silver beet is a highly perishable vegetable and should ideally be harvested ten minutes prior to being on the table.

CULTIVATION Prepare the bed by applying a complete fertiliser prior to sowing at the rate of 10 g per square metre. Sow seed in punnets or into garden drills. Select the strongest plants as transplants and place at 30 cm intervals. Protect young plants from birds — silver beet and lettuce are enticing as they are often the first leafy greens to appear in spring.

Well-drained soil and ample water are essential to the successful cultivation of silver beet. It also needs nitrogenous fertiliser to support the towering heads of leaf and welcomes poultry manure generously forked into the surrounding topsoil. Silver beet must be harvested from the outside inwards. Never pull leaves or take them from the centre without first removing older leaves.

SILVER BEET IS ONE OF THE HANDIEST CUT-AND-COME-AGAIN VEGETABLES.

In rainy weather, light mulching of the soil prevents mud splash on the underside of leaves. Leaves sometimes wilt in the midday sun even after a generous hosing. They recover in the cool evening and do not seem toughened by this experience.

VARIETIES 'Fordhook Giant' with broad white stems and dark green leaves is a popular and reliable type. For more stunning cultivars consider 'Ruby Chard' with crimson stalks and bright green leaves and 'Rainbow Chard' with stems of purple, red, pink or yellow.

Spinach
(*Spinacia oleracea*)
CHENOPODIACEAE FAMILY

Spinach comes from the same family as silver beet and beetroot. Spinach is a herbaceous perennial grown as an annual; it forms a rosette of leaves on a very short stem which later produces a flowering stalk bearing clusters of small, green, male and female flowers. Leaves may be smooth and arrow-shaped or broad and wrinkled (savoyed) depending on the cultivar. The leaves are a rich source of vitamins and can be lightly boiled or steamed or used in soups and stews.

CULTIVATION Spinach is a cool-season, 'short-day' plant and is best adapted to mild temperate and cold climates. The cooler temperate and mild inland elevated regions of Australia and most regions of New Zealand are suitable areas for cultivation. Plants grown in warm weather and under long day-length conditions tend to bolt and run to seed prematurely. Some hybrids now available may be grown in warmer areas.

Spinach plants thrive in soil that is given abundant water but is well drained. A light soil high in organic matter and nutrients is ideal. A pH of 6.0–6.5 is necessary. Measure the pH before planting and if acidic work lime into the top few centimetres of the bed several weeks before sowing. Enrich the soil with well-rotted animal manure or compost to provide a friable structure with good moisture-holding capacity.

Growing Hints

Plant Sow seed direct late summer, autumn or winter. Germinating temperature 5–25°C.
Harvest 8–10 weeks from sowing seed.
Fertilise Use liquid foliar spray or nitrogenous side dressing.
Planting for Average Family 10 plants.
Pests and Diseases Leaf miner, caterpillars, leaf spot, mildew.

Sowing time varies from autumn to spring depending on climate and type of spinach used, but hot weather during the growing season should always be avoided. In temperate climates begin sowing in early autumn. In colder regions sow from early autumn through winter to early spring. Seeds germinate well at low temperature (12–15°C). After scattering a pre-planting fertiliser (NPK 5:7:4) sow seed directly into the garden in rows 30 cm apart and 1–2 cm deep. Cover with a sandy soil mixture, compost or vermiculite and water gently. Seedlings are relatively slow to emerge (14 to 21 days). When they are 5–7 cm tall, thin seedlings to 15 cm within the rows.

Like other leafy vegetables, spinach must be grown quickly. It is a naturally quick-maturing crop and tends to bolt. Plants require regular watering, and weekly applications of liquid foliar fertiliser will benefit growth. Side dressings of nitrogenous fertiliser are a suitable alternative. Sulphate of ammonia gets a good response from the plants, ensuring a deep green leaf colour.

It is possible to harvest leaves eight to ten weeks after sowing. Pick the outside leaves progressively at ground level and new leaves will continue to grow. Warm weather, however, will hinder the cut-and-come-again nature of spinach. The plants can be cut off at ground level when fully grown.

For the average family requirements, ten plants are sufficient. Successive sowings at intervals of three or four weeks during the season can be made to prolong the harvest time.

VARIETIES 'English Hybrid' ('Winter Hybrid'); 'Hybrid 102'; 'Hybrid No. 7'.

Pods and Seeds

Vegetables grown for their pods or half-ripe seeds are predominantly members of the family Fabaceae. An outsider to this group is sweet corn (from the grass family) which is grown for its immature seeds.

With the exception of broad beans and peas, all the species are warm season plants so they should not be started too early in spring or too late in summer.

In pod and seed vegetables — unless harvested as dry seeds — the texture, flavour and food value depends on picking them at the right time. This applies especially to French beans, which ripen quickly in warm weather, and to peas in which sugar changes to starch as they mature. The conversion time from sugar to starch in sweet corn is even more critical as this change can take place after the cobs are picked. Fortunately, the ripening process in all pod and seed vegetables can be delayed by low temperature storage in the refrigerator for several days.

Beans
(*Phaseolus vulgaris*)
FABACEAE FAMILY

Beans are an important food crop which can be manipulated to yield handsomely over spring to early winter depending on local climate. A backyard garden can supply green, butter or wax beans, stringed or stringless, 5–60 cm long, over many months in great quantity. There are early- and late-

BEANS ARE REWARDING TO GROW, BEING ATTRACTIVE IN FLOWER AND PROVIDING A HEAVY CROP OF PODS. THERE IS A VAST ARRAY FROM WHICH TO CHOOSE — FRENCH DWARF OR CLIMBING, GREEN OR YELLOW PODS, SCARLET RUNNER BEANS OR BROAD BEANS — BRINGING GREAT VARIETY TO THE TABLE.

maturing varieties, many of them resistant to fungal and bacterial diseases. With the exception of the broad bean, all beans are warm weather crops.

CULTIVATION All types of French beans — dwarf or climbing, string or stringless — are warm season plants which are frost-susceptible. In subtropical and tropical regions, beans can be grown year-round bar the wet monsoonal season. In temperate climates sow from spring to late summer. In cold climates, the growing season is shorter and seed should be sown in spring. As the season grows warmer, crops have a shorter maturing time.

Beans must have adequate water with effective soil drainage. Wet feet, cold snaps

Yields

Climbing beans give heavier yields, longer crops, easier harvesting and more efficient use of space in the garden than bush beans. However, both bush beans and climbers can be encouraged to increase yields if beans are harvested at a slightly immature stage and are picked regularly.

and extreme heat can all reduce pod setting. Flower drop can also occur in climatic extremes. Both dwarf and climbing beans are susceptible to severe wind. Hot dry winds not only damage leaves and tug at the roots but may also cause faulty pollination of flowers and poor pod setting. So select a sheltered bed in the garden to avoid these problems. A sunny aspect is preferable.

Beans prefer a friable, moderately fertile soil. Crops may perform poorly on very sandy soils which lose moisture and nutrients quickly. Add compost or well-rotted animal manure to improve these soils. Phosphorus is an important nutrient and can be added as a pre-planting fertiliser (NPK 5:7:4) or as superphosphate. On acidic soils, add lime to raise the pH to 6.0–7.0.

Having regard to different climatic zones, in general sow seeds directly into the garden in spring after the last frost and when the soil has warmed. Seeds are susceptible to damping off fungus, so dust seeds with a fungicide before sowing. Some packet seeds may have already been chemically treated, making dusting unnecessary.

Bean seeds are liable to fertiliser burn if they come into direct contact with it. Preferably make two furrows 10–15 cm deep and scatter the pre-planting fertiliser along the bottom of each. Cover the soil and make a shallow seed furrow 4–5 cm deep between them. Insert the seeds 10 cm apart. Cover the seed furrow with soil, tamp it down and rake the bed level. If soil is just damp when sowing, no further watering will be necessary until the seedlings emerge in

seven to ten days. If making successive sowings, make the next sowing when seedlings in the previous one have formed their first true leaf.

Beans are an easy crop to grow and need little attention other than regular watering. At flowering, overhead watering will create a humid microclimate and improve pod setting. In addition, mulching around the plants and between the rows will prevent moisture loss and keep the roots cool.

Subsequent fertilising is usually unnecessary provided a pre-planting fertiliser has been incorporated. However, if plants are backward give a side dressing of complete fertiliser (NPK 10:4:6) or liquid feeds of water-soluble fertiliser at flowering time.

Dwarf beans are ready to pick in eight to ten weeks from sowing. Climbing beans take a week or two longer but yield a heavier crop and keep bearing for several weeks, often followed by a second flush of flowers. Start picking when the pods are young and tender before the seeds become too large. Pods ripen quickly; harvest every four or five days. Once the beans have cropped, maintain continuous picking as this prolongs the life of the plant and more beans are produced.

VARIETIES French beans are 15–25 cm long and usually green in colour. Some cultivars have yellow or wax pods (butter beans) and a few have purple pods which turn green when cooked. The pods can be string or stringless (snap) according to the amount of fibre at the junction.

French beans also vary in growth habit. Dwarf or bush beans are 40–50 cm tall while climbing or pole beans may grow 2–3 m tall and need a trellis or stakes to support the long twining stems.

In the dwarf or bush bean group, the most widely grown green string cultivars are 'Brown Beauty', 'Hawkesbury Wonder' and 'Windsor Long Pod'. 'Pencil Pod Black Wax', 'Butter Wax', and 'Sylvan Gold' are string, wax-pod cultivars.

Among the stringless dwarf beans are 'Tendergreen', 'Tendercrop', 'Redlands Pioneer', 'Apollo', 'Gourmet's Delight' and 'Limelight'. 'Bountiful Butter' and 'Cherokee Wax' are the best of the stringless wax pods.

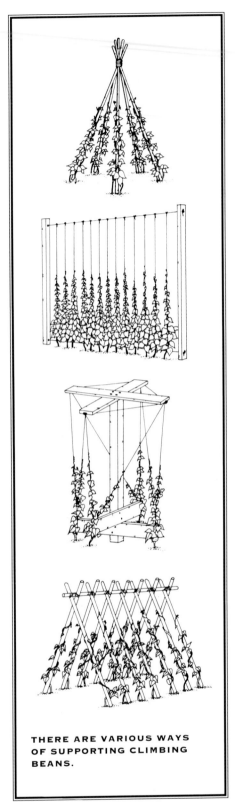

THERE ARE VARIOUS WAYS OF SUPPORTING CLIMBING BEANS.

In the climbing string-bean group, 'Epicure' and 'Westralia' (rust resistant) are the leading green pod beans. 'Purple King' with purple pods is also a recommended home garden bean. Stringless climbing beans with green pods are 'Blue Lake' which is best adapted to cool upland

BROAD BEANS ARE SOWN IN AUTUMN TO GROW THROUGH THE COOLER MONTHS.

climates and 'Giant of Stuttgart'. 'Golden Lake' and 'Golden Crop' are the best of the climbing stringless wax pod cultivars.

Beans, Broad (*Vicia faba*)

FABACEAE FAMILY

Unlike the other beans, the broad bean is a winter vegetable sown in the warmer areas in autumn and early winter and harvested in winter. It grows well in colder areas also but sets seed later and matures in spring.

The pods may contain eight to nine oblong seeds (longpod varieties) or four to five large round seeds (windsor varieties). The pods may be picked when quite small (5–7 cm) and sliced and cooked like French beans but they are usually picked later when they are well filled and the immature seeds are shelled like peas. Mature seeds can also be used as dry beans which are soaked to soften for cooking.

CULTIVATION Broad beans are best adapted to mild temperate and cold climates. The plant prefers a well-limed and sharply drained soil with reasonable fertility, a sunny aspect and ample water during the growing season. A high level of phosphorus in the soil is desirable. Too much nitrogen is detrimental as it promotes excessive leaf growth at the expense of flowers and pods. As legumes, broad beans have their own built-in nitrogen supply through their association with nodule bacteria in the roots and are a useful green manure crop.

Make furrows in rows at intervals of 60–70 cm. It is important that the newly sown seeds do not come in contact with fertiliser so place the required pre-planting fertiliser (NPK 5:7:4) in a deeper furrow on either side of the main furrow. Additional fertiliser is not usually necessary while the crop is growing.

Soil should be just damp at sowing time. Sow seeds directly into the garden 4–5 cm deep and 15 cm apart. Place them into the bottom of the furrow; cover the seed furrow with soil, firm it down and rake the surface level. When sown into damp soil, there is no

need for extra watering until the seedlings emerge in eight to fourteen days.

Tall varieties of broad beans require support against strong winds. Drive in 1 m high stakes at intervals along each row and stretch garden twine at a height of 30 cm between them. Use a second tier of twine at a height of 60 cm when the plants are tall enough. Also, cultivate between the rows and hill the plants at the same time for additional support.

To harvest, pick the pods before the beans harden and become floury. Immature pods have the best flavour and can be sliced and eaten like French beans. Regular picking encourages further pods to set.

VARIETIES 'Easy Long Pod'; 'Cole's Dwarf Prolific'; 'Green Windsor'; 'Cambridge Crimson'.

Beans, Runner (*Phaseolus coccineus*)

FABACEAE FAMILY

Runner beans (scarlet runner beans) are perennial climbers which grow during summer and die back in autumn to shoot again from the rootstock in spring. However, they are best grown as annuals from seed sown in spring or early summer. The twining vines reach 3 m and should be grown on a trellis or on stakes 2 m tall. Pinch out the tips of

Growing Hints

Plant Sow seed direct in
spring/early summer.
Harvest 8–12 weeks.
Fertilise As for beans.
Planting for Average Family
One 2 m long row.
Pests and Diseases As for beans.

Growing Hints

Plant Sow seed direct in spring
and summer.
Harvest 12–16 weeks after
sowing.
Fertilise Supplement base
fertilising with side dressings of a
complete fertiliser with a high
nitrogen content.
Planting for Average Family
20–25 plants.
Pests and Diseases Corn ear worm,
snails, slugs, aphids.

the leading shoots when they reach the top of the support. The pods are broader than French beans and have a slightly rough surface but are very tender when young with a distinctive flavour. The large seeds may be pink (often spotted or blotched with black) or white.

CULTIVATION Runner beans are widely grown in colder regions with mild summers; they are not recommended for hot climates.

Apart from their climatic limitations, runner beans thrive when given similar soil, fertiliser and cultural conditions to those of climbing French beans. A strong trellis is required to support the vigorous vines. Sow seeds in a double row (one each side of the trellis), spaced 15–25 cm apart. Take the usual precautions to avoid direct contact of seeds and fertiliser, and avoid overwatering after sowing. Dust seeds with fungicide to prevent damping off.

VARIETIES 'Scarlet Runner'; 'Streamline'; 'White Dutch'; 'White Zenith'.

Corn, Sweet
(*Zea mays*)
POACEAE FAMILY

A crop of sweet corn occupies a good deal of garden space but it is delicious when home-grown. It is easy to cultivate and highly nutritious. Desirable types of corn will have about 18 rows of grain on the cob and one or two cobs per plant.

CULTIVATION Sound bed preparation with applications of organic matter and complete fertiliser with a high nitrogen content are necessary. Liberal amounts of water are also required to grow corn successfully.

As corn is pollinated by wind, ensure maximum fertilisation by sowing seeds on a 25–30 cm grid: growing in blocks rather than rows aids wind pollination. Early sowings in spring should be no deeper than 3 cm while later sowings may be planted to a 5 cm depth. Plant two or three seeds together and thin to the strongest seedling.

Corn plants bear male flowers at the top of the plant and female flowers, or silk, lower down. Pollination occurs when pollen falls on the silk. Gently shaking the plant will loosen pollen and hasten fertilisation. Cobs are enclosed in husks from which the silk protrudes. When the silk browns it is time to harvest cobs while the grain is still full of opaque milky fluid. If left too long the kernels will turn starchy. The cobs should be used as soon as possible after picking.

VARIETIES 'Iochief' is an old reliable variety. 'Breakthrough F1' is a very sweet flavoured corn developed by Australian breeders. 'Micropops F1' is a baby corn which can be harvested when 2–4 cm in length and is excellent for Chinese cooking.

Peas (*Pisum sativum*)
FABACEAE FAMILY

Peas are sparse croppers compared with beans, giving only a few pickings per plant. While peas grow throughout summer in cool areas, they must be matured before the heat arrives in more northerly regions. Damage to flowers is caused by frosty weather and seed may be slow to germinate in cool, wet weather.

CULTIVATION Temperature is an important consideration when cultivating peas. They will not crop in the heat of the summer and frost will destroy flowers and therefore lower yields. The ideal soil is deep, well prepared and well drained, with a pH between 6.0 and 6.5.

Phosphorus is important in pea culture and can be added at the bed-preparation stage as a complete fertiliser (NPK 5:7:4) or as superphosphate at the rate of 10 g per running metre. Peas should not come into direct contact with fertiliser. Make two furrows 10–15 cm deep and scatter the pre-planting fertiliser along the bottom of each. Cover with soil and make a shallow seed furrow 4–5 cm deep between them. Sow seed directly into the garden at 5 cm intervals. Cover the seed furrow with soil,

Growing Hints

Plant Sow seed direct in late
winter; frost during flowering
period will harm crops so sow
late enough to avoid this.
Ideal germination temperature
is 22°C.
Harvest 12–16 weeks.
Fertilise Add complete fertiliser
high in phosphate during ground
preparation.
Planting for Average Family
Plant two 3 m rows at 14 day
intervals to give successive
cropping.
Pests and Diseases Red spider,
aphids, root rot, leaf and pod
spot. Poor germination caused by
fungi especially in cold, wet soil;
use pre-sowing dust.

tamp it down and rake the bed level. Peas sown in moist soil should not need watering until the seedlings appear. Overwatering will cause the peas to rot.

Careful shallow hoeing will control weeds. Support will be required for some varieties. Several wires or strings supported at each end of rows 3 m long and running right around the rows will hold up all but tall-growing varieties. Climbing peas which crop for a longer period need a sturdy trellis similar to that used for climbing beans.

To harvest, pull pods before the colour lightens and when the peas are fully grown but still tender. Successive weekly sowings can be made of quick-maturing types.

VARIETIES 'Greenfeast' is a reliable cultivar of the traditional pea. 'Telephone' is a good climbing variety.

Pea, Snow and Sugar Snap (*Pisum sativum*)

FABACEAE FAMILY

The snow pea and sugar snap pea are two strains of *Pisum sativum,* the garden pea. The snow pea (*P.s.* var. *macrocarpon*) is a distinct variety of garden pea while the sugar snap pea is a cross between

---

Growing Hints

Plant Sow seed direct in early to late winter in coastal areas and late winter through spring in cooler elevated areas.
Harvest 12–16 weeks depending on when seed was sown.
Fertilise Require phosphorus and to a lesser degree, nitrogen.
Planting for Average Family One 4–5 m row.
Pests and Diseases Red spider, aphids, root rot, leaf and pod spot.

---

the snow pea and another pea. Both are much prized in Asian cooking.

CULTIVATION Edible podded peas perform well under cool, moist conditions. They are sensitive to heat, and temperatures above 30°C will reduce yields. Frost will also adversely affect crops if it occurs during the flowering stage.

Cultivation is similar to the common green pea.

Harvesting time of snow peas is important. The pods should be of maximum size but with no development of seeds. Sugar snap peas are picked when the pods are fully developed and are like a normal garden pea in appearance.

VARIETIES Snow Peas: 'Prolific'; 'Snowflake'; 'Sweet Rod'; 'Mammoth Melting Sugar'; 'Bikini'. Sugar Snap: 'Sugar Bon'; 'Sugar Anne'; 'Honeypod'; 'Sugar Snap Climbing'; 'Dwarf Sugar Snap'.

Roots

Most of the root vegetables — beetroot, carrot, parsnip, turnip and swede — are biennials which develop a large taproot in the first season from which flowering stalks are produced in the second season. For this reason, these root crops tend to bolt or run to seed prematurely if their seeds are sown out of season. Radish, the only annual root vegetable, may also run to seed if the roots remain in the soil too long.

Most are cool or intermediate season crops and grow best in cool to mild temperatures. Some can also be cultivated during summer.

Root vegetables require a light, friable, well-drained soil which allows the storage organs to develop evenly and smoothly. Seeds of root vegetables are sown directly into the garden because seedlings transplant badly.

As a rule root crops should follow leaf crops which have been heavily manured. Fresh manure must not be used on root crops, otherwise there is a tendency for the plants to develop forked or misshapen roots. They can also follow any fruit crops that have been heavily manured and, about ten days prior to sowing, work in a dressing of a low-nitrogen, high-phosphorus, high-potassium plant food.

These vegetables should not be over-fertilised with nitrogen which promotes too much leaf growth at the expense of the roots. Provided a pre-planting fertiliser (NPK 5:7:4) has been applied before sowing, extra fertiliser is rarely needed.

IVY HANSEN

PICK SNOW PEAS WHEN PODS ARE OF MAXIMUM SIZE BUT BEFORE THE DEVELOPMENT OF SEEDS.

ROOT CROPS SUCH AS BEETROOT, TURNIPS AND PARSNIPS ARE BEST DIRECT SEEDED IN THE BED IN WHICH THEY ARE TO GROW.

IVY HANSEN

As a group, root vegetables keep much better in storage than those grown for their fruit, pods, leaves and stems. However, storage ability depends largely on the maturity of the tubers at harvest time. Roots which take longer to grow store better than early-maturing cultivars.

Beetroot (*Beta vulgaris*)

CHENOPODIACEAE FAMILY

Beetroot varies in shape from round or globe-shaped to oblong or tube-shaped according to variety. Beetroot is one of the easiest vegetables to grow and is particularly delicious when picked young and used as baby beets.

Beetroot is a very salt-tolerant crop and may be irrigated using water with a high saline content.

CULTIVATION Although basically a cool-season crop there are beetroot varieties available which will prosper in all but extreme climatic zones. In subtropical and tropical regions, sow seed in almost any month of the year, avoiding only the wet summer season in the tropics. In temperate and cold climates, sow from early spring to early autumn. Later sowing in cooler temperatures may cause the plants to run to seed with little or no root development.

Beetroot thrives in most well-drained soils. Although the globe sits only partly in the soil, beetroots need the same moderate fertilising as other root crops to prevent forking. On heavy soils incorporate organic matter, either animal manure or garden compost in moderate amounts to improve soil structure. If the soil is very acidic add lime when preparing the bed to bring the pH to between 6.5 and 7.0. Too much lime, however, may cause a deficiency of manganese and boron.

Sowing seed directly in to the garden is the preferred method of propagation as transplants are not always successful. Scatter a pre-planting fertiliser (NPK 5:7:4) in a band where seed is to be sown in rows 20–30 cm apart and rake it into the surface soil. Make 12 mm deep furrows with a rake handle in just-damp soil. Sow seed in the drills and cover with a sandy soil mix, garden compost or vermiculite. Mulch lightly and keep bed in a damp condition until seedlings emerge in about two weeks. Thin plants to 10 cm apart.

Cultivate between rows to control weeds but do not hill up the soil around the plants. Nitrogenous foliar sprays will promote quick growth and tender roots if applied at two week intervals after the globes begin to swell.

Beetroots are at their best and full of sugar when just short of maturity. Start pulling alternate roots early, eight to ten weeks from sowing seeds. This spreads the harvest and allows more space for the remaining roots to grow. Globes 5–7 cm in diameter are an ideal size; larger roots may become tough and stringy.

For the average family's needs, successive sowings of 2–3 m rows can be made monthly during the season.

Bleeding

Most beets will bleed into the cooking water no matter how much care is taken to prevent bruising and cutting. Bleeding may be reduced by screwing off the tops leaving 3–5 cm of stem and all of the roots.

Growing Hints

Plant Sow seeds direct year round in mild climates.
Harvest 10–12 weeks from sowing seed, 6–8 weeks from seedlings.
Fertilise Apply nitrogenous foliar spray.
Planting for Average Family Sow one 3 m row progressively.
Pests and Diseases Well-managed beet rarely attracts pests; aphids leaf spot and leaf miner may be troublesome.

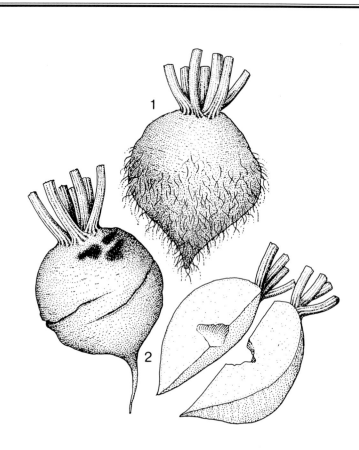

1 Heavy or new manure on beetroot beds will result in hairy or distorted roots of inferior texture. Always sow beetroot in a bed that was heavily manured for a previous crop.
2 Cracks, dark spots and hollow heart inside beetroot indicate boron deficiency. When beetroot seedlings are 10 cm high, spray with liquid fertiliser containing all the trace elements.

VARIETIES 'Derwent Globe'; 'Early Market'; 'Green Top Bunching' and 'Emerald' are excellent globe-shaped varieties for the home garden. 'Long Pickling' or 'Cylindrica' are the best of the long, tube-shaped varieties — their roots are 15 cm long and 5 cm in diameter.

'Baby Beets' and 'Mini Gourmet Beetroot' are available in seed packets and are becoming popular served whole as a side dish. Both cultivars are flavoursome and attractive mini vegetables.

Novelty varieties include 'Golden Beet' and 'Golden Apollo' with bright yellow flesh; 'Snow White' with white flesh; and 'Italian Chioggia' with concentric rings of pink and white.

Carrot
(*Daucus carota*)

APIACEAE FAMILY

Carrots are a favourite home-grown vegetable. Although a cool-season plant, they are climatically adaptable and have a long cropping period. Depending on the variety, roots may be long and tapering or shorter with a rounded end. Others are cylindrical or globe-shaped. A deep orange colour is preferred but there are a few varieties with cream, yellow or purple flesh.

CULTIVATION Carrots are very temperature-tolerant but germination cannot be achieved in cold soil. In warm northern regions, sow seed in most months of the year, avoiding only the hot, wet season from December to March. In temperate and cold climates, sow seed from early spring through to autumn. Provide a sunny position where warm air and soil temperatures will prevail to ensure good growth and development. The carotene in carrots, which determines the depth of orange colour, is influenced to a certain extent by temperature. Carrots grown in temperatures of 16–21°C will have good root colour while those grown at temperatures above or below this range will usually have poorer colour. The colour is also determined by the cultivar.

Carrots will grow in a wide variety of soils and depths providing they are in good tilth, well-drained, have a pH of 6.0–6.5 and receive ample water, especially after the roots have become well established. The ideal soil type is a deep, sandy loam or alternatively heavier soils with a good structure which allow the roots to grow and expand quickly. On shallow soils, select varieties of carrot with short rather than long, tapering roots. Heavy soils produce more misshapen roots than those of lighter or more open texture, so improve clay soils by adding coarse sand and organic matter.

Do not grow carrots in the same location more than once every 3–4 years as disease organisms affecting carrots can carry over in the soil. Carrots thrive in soils which have been heavily manured and fertilised by a previous crop. A space last used by an unrelated leaf crop is ideal.

Like all root crops, carrots can be subject to deformity if planted into soil newly fertilised with fresh animal manure. Instead of manure, use a pre-planting fertiliser (NPK 5:7:4) for bed preparation. The soil must be in crumbly, friable condition for direct sowing. Scatter the fertiliser in a band where seeds are to be sown and rake it into the topsoil. Make shallow furrows 12 mm deep by pressing a rake handle into a just damp surface. Space the furrows 20–30 cm apart for most varieties. Reduce this spacing to 10–15 cm for small varieties.

Sow seed directly into the furrows or drills by drizzling the seed mixed with sand for even distribution. Cover with compost, vermiculite or a sandy soil mixture. Scatter a light mulch on the bed to prevent the surface soil caking and to retain moisture. Keep the bed damp but not wet with light watering until the seedlings emerge — ten days in warm soil. Weed control is essential but cultivation must be shallow.

Ruthless thinning must be practised with the first weeding. At the first thinning, discard the smallest plants to leave a 2 cm radius about each remaining plant. Make a second thinning to 5 cm apart when seedlings are 15 cm tall. Remove further weeds at the same time. The young roots from the second thinning may be large enough to eat. Usually small varieties need thinning only once. As the plants grow, cultivate between rows and hill the soil slightly to the roots. If a mulch is then scattered between the rows, further weeding is unnecessary.

Additional fertiliser is seldom required if a pre-planting fertiliser has been applied. If plants are not growing adequately, give liquid feeds of water-soluble fertilisers but do not overfeed especially with nitrogen. Watering should be even. Alternating wet and dry soil can lead to cracking of the root.

It is possible to have several successive crops of carrots through spring, summer and autumn. Most varieties take 16–20 weeks from sowing to harvest but small baby carrots may be ready in 10–12 weeks. Pull the carrots before they get too old as they may become tough and woody. Soil should be damp when harvesting so that the roots lift cleanly and the tops do not break. On heavy soil, loosen the roots with a garden fork but take care not to damage them.

VARIETIES   'Western Red' is the dominant variety. 'Topweight' and 'All Seasons' have long tapering roots. All are

Growing Hints

Plant Sow seed direct, successively through spring, summer and autumn.
Harvest 16–20 weeks from sowing.
Fertilise Apply light nitrogenous foliar spray.
Planting for Average Family One 4 m row with successive sowings at intervals of 4–5 weeks during the growing season.
Pests and Diseases Vegetable weevil, aphids, nematodes, carrot or motley dwarf virus (resistant varieties available).

THERE ARE CARROT VARIETIES TO SUIT ALL CLIMATES AND SOIL TYPES. CHOOSE VARIETIES WITH LONG TAPERING ROOTS FOR DEEP SOILS AND SHORTER, STUMP-ROOTED TYPES FOR SHALLOW SOILS.

virus-resistant.

The 'Chantenay' group has stump roots. 'Onward' is a new stump root variety with some virus resistance.

Finger or baby carrots are becoming increasingly popular and are excellent choices for container culture. 'Amsterdam Forcing', 'Baby', 'Five Star Baby' and 'Short and Sweet' produce cylindrically shaped roots 7–10 cm long. 'Tom Thumb' and 'Mini Round' produce small round roots.

Ginger
(*Zingiber officinale*)

ZINGIBERACEAE FAMILY

Ginger is indispensable in Chinese cooking. Although strictly a herb, it can be easily incorporated into the vegetable garden. It is a rhizomatous perennial with the aerial parts growing up to 60 cm high. It requires tropical conditions to be grown outdoors. In cool or temperate regions it must be grown in a warm glasshouse.

CULTIVATION A shaded position and well-drained loam enriched with organic matter are essential for good growth. pH in the range 5.5–7.0 is suitable — very acidic soils can be limed using up to 300 g per square metre. Incorporate a pre-planting fertiliser as ginger is a heavy feeder.

Growing Hints

Plant Rhizomes planted in early spring.
Harvest By mid-March to avoid too much fibre in the roots: about 8 months.
Fertilise Use a complete fertiliser at bed-preparation stage; monthly side dressings of highly nitrogenous fertilisers.
Planting for Average Family 1 plant.
Pests and Diseases Not troubled.

Propagation is achieved from pieces of rhizome bearing one or more leaf buds — the more buds the greater the yield of ginger. Ginger roots sold at greengrocers are suitable for planting provided they are fresh and plump.

Plant rhizomes in spring with the top 2–3 cm below the soil surface spaced 15–20 cm apart.

After planting, water the bed and mulch 7–8 cm deep. Avoid overwatering but keep soil damp. Wind protection is advisable. Harvest in winter after the leaves have died down.

Kohlrabi (*Brassica oleracea* var. *gongylodes*)

BRASSICACEAE FAMILY

Kohlrabi is a strange member of the brassicas, being half cabbage and half turnip. The stem swells at ground level to form a ball from which long-stemmed leaves emerge. It can be eaten raw or cooked.

CULTIVATION Kohlrabi is a cool-season vegetable. While hardier than most brassicas such as cauliflower, kohlrabi requires identical bed preparation and

---

Growing Hints

Plant Sow seed in late summer and autumn.
Harvest 12–14 weeks from seed; 8–10 weeks from seedlings (late winter and spring).
Fertilise Apply complete fertiliser as base dressing and nitrogenous foliar feeds or side dressings.
Planting for Average Family 15–20 plants.
Pests and Diseases Grey aphids, white butterfly, cabbage moth, cutworms, black beetle, downy mildew, club root, black rot.

---

responds to the same feeding. Young kohlrabi is delicate in flavour and crisply succulent. The rank and fibrous nature of overgrown kohlrabi, however, has tended to give the plant a poor culinary reputation.

Plant directly in drills at 20 cm intervals with rows 30 cm apart. Harvest while still young and tender. The edible part of the plant develops above the ground. It should be cut when the swollen stem is 5 cm in diameter. Allowing plants to over-mature will cause woodiness.

VARIETIES 'White Vienna', 'Early Purple', 'Purple Vienna'.

Parsnip
(*Pastinaca sativa*)

APIACEAE FAMILY

Parsnips are biennial plants which form a rosette of compound leaves and a fleshy taproot 15–30 cm long. The roots are white or cream with a characteristic flavour. Roots may be boiled, baked or fried, or chopped into pieces for use in soups and stews.

Parsnips are easy to grow and the plant is hardy but it requires a long, cool season to develop.

CULTIVATION Parsnips grow well in southwestern and eastern Australia and most regions of New Zealand. They require the same conditions as carrots. In warm

---

Growing Hints

Plant Sow seed direct from spring, through summer and into early autumn.
Harvest 18–20 weeks.
Fertilise Apply light nitrogenous foliar sprays.
Planting for Average Family One 3 m drill sown every 4–6 weeks.
Pests and Diseases Aphids, nematodes, vegetable weevil, powdery mildew, leaf spot.

---

regions, sow seed from late summer through to the following spring. In temperate and cold climates, sow from early spring to early autumn.

For best results soil should be deeply dug, well drained and in an area that has been heavily fertilised from a previous, unrelated crop. Organic matter, if worked into the bed well beforehand, will not cause misshapen roots. Scatter a pre-planting fertiliser (NPK 5:7:4) in a band 15 cm wide where seeds are to be sown and rake it into the topsoil.

The viability of the seed deteriorates rapidly if kept for more than a year so use fresh seed. Even new packs can be disappointing, so make drill sowings thick to ensure a sufficient strike.

Sow seeds directly into drills 1–1.5 cm deep and 30 cm apart. Cover the seed lightly and scatter a thin mulch over the bed. Water gently. Keep the soil damp until the seedlings emerge in 15–20 days.

When plants are 5 cm high, thin out to 8 cm apart. Parsnips do not compete well against weeds. Control by shallow cultivation between the rows or hand weed. Extra fertiliser is seldom necessary, however, should the plants fail to thrive when the roots start to form, a side dressing of fertiliser (NPK 5:7:4) will promote faster growth and better quality roots. Do not overfeed plants with highly nitrogenous fertilisers.

Although the shoot system is frost-susceptible, the flavour of the roots is in fact improved by frost. Parsnip roots reach maturity in four to five months but it is advisable to start digging them earlier to spread the harvest. When the soil is damp loosen the roots with a fork so that they lift without breaking.

Successive sowings at intervals of five or six weeks can be made.

VARIETIES 'Hollow Crown'.

Radish
(*Raphanus sativus*)

BRASSICACEAE FAMILY

The radish is the quickest growing vegetable and the easiest of all to grow

THE EDIBLE PART OF KOHLRABI DEVELOPS ABOVE THE GROUND.

— an excellent beginner's choice. Radishes come in different shapes and sizes and may be divided into two groups: quick-growing small radishes and large winter radishes which take two to three months to mature. The small radishes may be round to long and tapering and either red or white, while winter radishes are generally long and tapering or cylindrical, and red, white or dark skinned. Early-maturing cultivars with small, round roots are ideal plants for growing in containers.

CULTIVATION Radishes must be grown quickly to achieve the best flavour

RADISHES ARE THE QUICKEST AND EASIEST CROP TO GROW — A GOOD BEGINNER'S CHOICE.

and texture. Slow growth results in bitter and woody roots. Early-maturing cultivars of radish can be grown in all climates at almost any time of the year. Winter radish cultivars are best grown in temperate and cold climates to mature in late autumn or winter.

Radishes require a rich soil, well manured from a previous crop. Light or sandy loams are ideal. The poorer the soil, the lower the quality of the radish. Their other main requirement is ample water during the growing period.

To ensure quick growth prepare the bed well with organic matter and a pre-planting fertiliser (NPK 5:7:4) scattered in a band where the seeds are to be sown. Sow seeds directly into shallow drills 15–20 cm apart. Cover the seeds with a sandy soil mixture, compost or vermiculite and water gently. Seeds germinate quickly and seedlings will emerge in about seven days, sometimes less. Thin the seedlings of small varieties to 3–5 cm intervals and those of the larger winter varieties to 5–7 cm.

Water regularly and give liquid feeds every 10 to 14 days to promote rapid growth.

To spread the harvest, start pulling the roots when large enough to use. If left in the soil too long, the roots become coarse and strongly flavoured. Successive plantings every three to four weeks will keep the family in radishes.

VARIETIES Round: 'Cherry Belle'; 'Red Prince'; 'Round Red'. Tankard: 'French Breakfast'. Tapering: 'Long Scarlet'; 'White Icicle'. Winter: 'China Rose'; 'Black Spanish'.

Growing Hints

Plant Sow seed direct; successive sowings year-round.
Harvest 4–6 weeks; winter radish 8–12 weeks.
Fertilise Apply complete fertiliser during ground preparation.
Planting for Average Family One 3 m row every 4 weeks.
Pests and Diseases Aphids, cabbage moth, white butterfly.

Swede (*Brassica napobrassica*)

BRASSICACEAE FAMILY

This problem-free winter root crop is a member of the cabbage family and should not succeed cabbage in the same garden space. Swede turnips are a larger vegetable than the ordinary turnip, with yellow flesh while the ordinary turnip is commonly white-fleshed. Both grow with their bulbous parts aboveground or only slightly underground, and when in prime condition their flesh is as crisp as apple. Both are frost-resistant.

CULTIVATION Sow swedes from late summer to autumn so that frosty winter conditions may put sweetness into the flesh. In cold climates seed may also be sown in late winter or early spring.

Prepare the soil well beforehand to have the bed in a damp, crumbly condition for direct sowing. On heavy clay soils add organic matter to improve structure, and if the soil is very acidic, add lime. Scatter the pre-planting fertiliser (NPK 5:7:4 or superphosphate) over the bed at the rate of 100 g per square metre, or band it along the line where seeds are to be sown. Rake the fertiliser into the topsoil and mark out seed furrows 12 mm deep.

To sow, scatter seed in drills and thin later to 5–10 cm interval depending on variety. Supplementary side dressings of nitrogenous fertiliser at a rate of 25 g per square metre need be given only if plants are slowing up.

Cultivate between rows to destroy weeds but do not hill the plants with soil because the roots are formed at soil level. The leafy canopy soon covers the inter-row space and this will discourage further weed growth. Water regularly.

Do not allow the roots to mature too long and achieve considerable size or they will become coarse and bitter. Small globes of 5 cm diameter are superior in flavour and texture.

VARIETIES 'Champion Purple Top' is the most favoured cultivar. Also available are 'Royal Rose' (or 'Tipperary') and 'Laing's Garden'.

Sweet Potato
(*Ipomoea batatas*)
CONVOLVULACEAE FAMILY

These perennials of the morning glory family have trailing vines bearing a dense mass of arrow-shaped leaves. The edible underground tubers may have creamy-white, buff, brown, pink or purple coloured skin. The flesh is usually white but some cultivars have yellow flesh. The vines are rambling and require a lot of space to grow.

As subtropical plants they need a warm climate with six frost-free months to grow properly. Areas with short summers rarely grow satisfactory sweet potatoes. This is a slow crop and it cannot be forced in less than the 18 to 20 weeks needed before it comes to harvest. Its cultivation is not recommended in cool temperate or cold regions.

CULTIVATION Deep, light soils or those enriched with organic matter to provide a friable crumb structure are most suitable. Soil which supported a previous leaf crop is excellent for sweet potatoes provided they are planted over a banding of superphosphate or complete fertiliser (NPK 5:7:4).

To prepare the bed spread the pre-planting fertiliser at the rate + 5 g to a metre along the line where the plants are to grow, rake it into the topsoil and form a ridge 10 cm above the garden bed for planting the shoots.

Propagation is by shoots or cuttings from tubers. Sweet potatoes are root tubers which produce new shoots at the top of the tuber. Shoots or cuttings may be available in late winter or early spring from nurseries. Alternatively, tubers can be purchased and buried in a box of moist sand. If kept in a warm spot, shoots will soon develop. When the shoots are 10–15 cm long, carefully separate them from the parent tuber for transplanting.

Plant shoots out allowing about 45 cm between plants within rows and 75 cm between rows, placing them close to the soil surface.

Carefully cultivate between plants and rows to control weeds until the vines cover the soil in between. During growth keep pulling in soil to cover the developing tubers. Water well once a week during dry spells. Lift runners up occasionally to prevent roots

developing at the nodes of the vines. New plants formed at the nodes restrict tuber development under the parent plant.

Additional fertiliser is rarely necessary if a preplanting fertiliser has been used. If plants are forced by overwatering and feeding, the tubers may become misshapen. When watering do so at regular intervals as uneven irrigation can lead to cracked roots.

Tubers are normally harvested before frosts occur but after the vine leaves have turned yellow. Tuber quality improves with maturity but if cold weather or frost is expected, harvest the tubers immediately. Tubers subjected to temperatures below 10°C will be damaged and will not store well. Dig the roots on a fine day, exposing them to the sun for two or three hours to dry completely before storing in a warm, dry, well-ventilated place. Before storing discard any tubers with blemishes or symptoms of rotting.

VARIETIES Recommended cultivars are 'White Maltese' (white flesh), 'Puerto Rico' (yellow flesh) and 'Centennial' (salmon flesh).

Turnip
(*Brassica rapa*)
BRASSICACEAE FAMILY

The edible, thick, globular turnip root has creamy white or yellow flesh and a

TURNIPS ARE USEFUL ADDITIONS TO SOUPS AND STEWS. GROW THEM QUICKLY — THEY ARE AT THEIR BEST WHEN PULLED AND EATEN JUST BEFORE MATURITY.

Early-maturing varieties will be ready to pull in five to ten weeks. Later maturing types should be forked up. Twist off the tops and store in sand in a cool, dry place.

To have a continuous crop, make successive plantings.

VARIETIES Recommended cultivars include 'Purple-top'; 'White Globe', with round roots with purple crowns; and 'White Stone' with rounded roots and white flesh of excellent quality.

A cultivar grown for both tops and roots is 'Foliage Turnip' or 'Shagoin'.

'Tokyo Cross F_1' is a quick-maturing cultivar with small white roots measuring 5 cm across.

Stems

Stem vegetables are those harvested for their stalks or petioles. They are a diverse group coming from a range of families.

Asparagus, celery and rhubarb all appreciate a well-prepared rich soil as they are greedy feeders. Apart from this there is little to tie them together with respect to cultivation and each should be viewed separately.

Asparagus (*Asparagus officinalis*)

LILLIACEAE FAMILY

Asparagus is a deep-rooted, herbaceous perennial grown for its tender, edible early spring shoots (spears) which arise from the subterranean crown. Although regarded as a luxury vegetable, it is easily grown in most friable soils. However, the production of choice spears demands care and knowledge. Asparagus produces male and female reproductive organs on separate plants. Male plants give the highest yields and crop earlier each season than the female plants which produce the largest spears. Growers prefer male plants, so ascertain whether male or female plants are on offer when purchasing rootstock. If sowing seed,

Growing Hints

Plant Sow seed directly into drills in summer and autumn.
Harvest 10–12 weeks (winter and early spring).
Fertilise Apply base fertiliser followed by side dressings if necessary.
Planting for Average Family 10–15 plants in successive sowings.
Pests and Diseases Aphids, cabbage moth, white butterfly, vegetable weevil.

mild taste. Turnips should not be confused with swede turnips which have a long neck or crown and a strong flavour.

Turnips are a frost-resistant, cool-season crop and require 12 weeks to grow.

CULTIVATION Turnips must be grown rapidly and are at their best when pulled and eaten just before full maturity. Propagate from seed sown directly into the garden in summer and autumn. Seedlings do not transplant well.

Any well-drained garden soil will support turnips. Sow seed 1 cm deep in rows 30 cm apart; at seedling stage thin to 5–7 cm apart. Water well during dry spells and liquid fertilise to keep them growing vigorously.

IVY HANSEN

CELERY, ASPARAGUS AND RHUBARB ARE ALL GROWN FOR THEIR EDIBLE STALKS OR PETIOLE.

the grower can select male plants in the second season.

CULTIVATION   For best results asparagus requires an annual dormant period. Regions with a definite winter are more suited to its culture than hot or temperate zones. Asparagus can be grown on the coast but it does not do as well as in elevated tableland areas.

As an asparagus bed will be productive for 15 odd years, it is important that the soil be deep, friable, reasonably fertile and well supplied with organic matter. It needs to be thoroughly tilled and have good drainage. A slightly acidic to neutral pH is ideal (pH 6.2–6.8). Apply lime to soil that is known to be very acidic.

In preparation set aside a permanent, sharply drained bed and dig to double spade depth without disturbing the subsoil. Enrich with the best growth-promoting materials available. Animal manure, compost and inorganic fertilisers are all useful for continued production. Adding a complete fertiliser (NPK 10:9:8) or Banana Special fertiliser gets the plants off to good growth and development. Till and retill to distribute the soil-building materials, and if the soil remains heavy add sand or peat to increase friability. Heavy soil results in bent asparagus spears.

Asparagus can be established by seed or crowns. Home gardeners often prefer direct seeding but as germination can be erratic several points must be observed. Only sow seed in well-drained, deep, alluvial or sandy loam soil with high fertility and organic content. Control weeds prior to sowing and work the soil into a fine tilth. There must be an adequate moisture content at sowing time and an optimum soil temperature of 25–30°C. Sow seed 20–30 mm deep with the first harvest of spears occurring in the third year.

The plant can also be established by planting one- or two-year-old crowns with strong undamaged roots. The older the crowns, the shorter the time needed before harvesting the crop. Plant the crowns by digging a 25 cm trench and mounding the bottom slightly. Set the crowns astride the mound and pull in the soil from the sides to cover to a depth of 5 cm, adding more soil as the young spears grow but do not completely cover them. Observe 60 cm intervals each way.

The first year's crop should be allowed to mature and go to fern. The slender wands can grow up to 25 m high before female plants go to seed in their second year, producing bright red seed berries. Female plants can be rogued as soon as their sex is disclosed because they are less prolific than the male. Always leave the fern to die before removing and burning, then level soil if hilling has been practised. Resist plundering the spears in their second year, except for taking a few of the choicest, thus allowing the crowns to build up strength.

Blanch asparagus if desired by forming a mound of soil 25–30 cm high over the rows before they emerge through the soil. Cut when they emerge. For green asparagus do not earth up and do not cut the spears until they are 18–23 cm above ground level.

Fertilising should consist of a side dressing of complete fertiliser high in nitrogen after harvesting. Simultaneously remove weeds and water as necessary to keep the soil moist.

Once the third year of growth has been reached full harvesting can begin. The bed will be productive for another 15 years and then it will take another three years to kill out the plants if the land is needed for another crop. In the third year, the first cutting of spears should be limited to between four and six weeks, but as the plants mature the harvesting period can be increased until a maximum of 12 weeks is achieved. To harvest, cut the spears, never pull them.

If the plants have been grown from seed, when the crowns form do not divide them or the plants will return to the yield of a third-year harvest. Allow crowns to multiply naturally.

VARIETIES 'Mary Washington'.

Growing Hints

Plant Seed sown in spring; crowns planted in winter.
Harvest In spring from the third year.
Fertilise Apply complete fertiliser high in nitrogen after harvest.
Planting for Average Family 12 plants.
Pests and Diseases Slugs, snails.

Celery (*Apium graveolens*)

APIACEAE FAMILY

Celery is a hungry, lime-loving vegetable, and it is generally best to devote space to a smaller number of plants rather than starve 15 to 20. It is grown for the edible leafstalk, or petiole, which by cultivation and blanching is reduced in acridity and becomes delicate and tender.

CULTIVATION Celery thrives in a climate with a long season of warm days and cool nights with medium to low humidity. It must be grown quickly to prevent stalks getting pithy. Low rainfall reduces disease problems but the crop will need to be irrigated.

Celery appreciates rich, moist but well-drained soil in a sunny position. An alluvial or peaty soil is ideal. Celery has a small root system in comparison with its aerial parts and is therefore water-hungry. An abundance of organic matter incorporated into the bed will ensure the balance of water-holding capacity and good drainage that is needed. A pH of between 5.5 and 6.5 is suitable. Soils with pH of less than 5.5 require liming, preferably with dolomite which contains magnesium.

Sow seeds in flats or punnets and later transplant to a permanent location. Take care not to disturb roots unduly when transplanting. Preferably, move only on a cool day or late in the evening when less transpiration from the plant itself will help prevent dehydration. Space the plants 30 cm within the row and 50 cm between rows.

Mulch heavily with rotted manure. Give some protection from frost and sun scald. Control weeds and apply ample water during dry spells.

Blanching (excluding light from the plant to reduce the green colouring) is practised by some gardeners. To do this, the stems can be wrapped in brown paper or corrugated cardboard or a piece of drainage pipe can be dropped over the plant. Close spacing will also shield out the light to some extent. The old practice of banking up the soil to blanch the plants has fallen from favour owing to the risk of introducing soil-borne diseases. Blanching aids are not required until three to four weeks before harvest.

Fertilisers must quickly reach the roots, so plants should be given plenty of liquid feeding. A weekly banding of a complete liquid fertiliser and a side dressing of animal manure is recommended. Poultry manure is excellent.

To harvest cut the stalks at soil level.

VARIETIES 'Crisp Salad'; 'Five Star Stringless'; 'Golden Self Blanching'; 'South Australian White'.

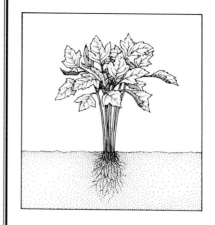

BLANCHING CELERY.

STEMS OF CELERY GROWN IN TRENCH MAY BE WRAPPED FOR BLANCHING.

Growing Hints

Plant Sow seed or plant seedlings in spring and summer.
Harvest After stems reach 15–20 cm in length (3 to 4 months after transplanting).
Fertilise Ensure rich pre-planting bed preparation and regular foliar feeds.
Planting for Average Family 10 plants.
Pests and Diseases Aphids, leaf spot.

Rhubarb
(*Rheum rhaponticum*)
POLYGONACEAE FAMILY

Rhubarb is a very useful vegetable for stewing and adding to pies. It grows well in areas with cool, moist summers and cold winters.

CULTIVATION Rhubarb will crop well for four or five years before needing to be divided. Soil fertility and bed preparation are therefore important. Well-drained, highly-fertile, friable soils are recommended. If necessary build up the bed, as rhubarb must be planted in well-drained soil; it resents waterlogging.

As rhubarb is a gross feeder, the beds should be well prepared with organic manure or compost as well as an all-round fertiliser worked into the top 30–40 cm. Additional fertilising is also necessary over the years but is usually of a surface nature.

Seed of the red-stalked rhubarb types can be sown in spring or summer, and as stalk colour varies the weaker and paler red seedlings can be discarded. However, it is quicker and easier to select the best crown from a clump of established rhubarb and divide this. Divide the clump in late winter or spring, making sure that each division has roots and at least one strong bud. Plant the crowns 1 m apart with each crown just above soil surface. Nurseries usually have crowns or young plants available during winter.

Rhubarb stalks may be fully harvested over six weeks in their third year of growth. In the first year after planting don't pick the stalks. This will allow the roots to enlarge. In the second year, harvest for two weeks only.

When the plants are in their third year and onwards and once full harvesting is established, pick the outside leaves progressively. One-third of the stalks should be allowed to remain on the plant after each harvest.

VARIETIES 'Sydney Crimson'; 'Wilson's Ruby'; 'Champagne'; 'Wandin Giant'.

Tubers

A tuber is a swollen portion of an underground stem or rhizome, serving as a storage organ for the plant by holding any excess carbohydrate produced. Ideal climatic conditions for

Harvesting Rhubarb

Rhubarb crowns can be set back by careless picking. Always harvest from the outside inwards, gently snapping off stems with a sideways tug. Harvest all thin stems so that the plants can get on with the job of producing thicker, longer ones.

Growing Hints

Plant Seed or crowns.
Harvest 16–20 weeks.
Fertilise Ensure initial bed preparation and annual side dressing with complete fertiliser.
Planting for Average Family 3–4 plants.
Pests and Diseases Downy mildew, root rot.

HARVEST RHUBARB STEMS FROM THE OUTSIDE INWARDS.

FRESHLY DUG POTATOES AND SWEET POTATOES WILL BE A WELCOME ADDITION TO THE KITCHEN TO ADD TO HEARTY WINTER SOUPS AND STEWS.

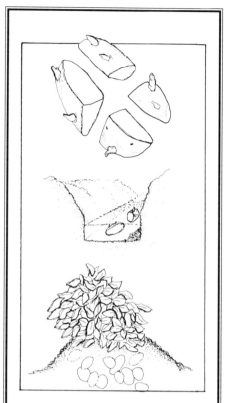

When preparing potato seed, cut tuber so each section has a couple of healthy eyes.
Place bands of fertiliser along each side of trench and cover with a thin layer of soil before placing seed potatoes in position. As plants grow, soil is hilled up around the potatoes to protect them from light and disease.

producing an excess of carbohydrate are mild, sunny days and cool nights, as photosynthesis will be high during the days and respiration will be minimal during the nights.

The Jerusalem artichoke is not fussy about soil, however, the potato is one of the very few vegetables that has a preference for slight acidity. A range of between pH 5.5 and 6.5 is suitable.

Potato (*Solanum tuberosum*)

SOLANACEAE FAMILY

The foodcrop gardener usually grows a few potatoes as a challenge. A small garden is unlikely to produce all of a household's needs, unless all of the available area is given over to the crop.

But even the occasional plant, allowed to prosper as it may, will yield a nest of lovely tubers if the soil is rich.

The potato plant is a herbaceous perennial with white or purplish flowers developing into a small, green berry. The plant has fibrous roots and many rhizomes or underground stems which become swollen at the tip to form the edible tubers. The tubers are also used for planting and are commonly referred to as 'seed potatoes'.

CULTIVATION Good potatoes are the result of careful soil preparation and suitable temperatures during cultivation. Although an adaptable crop, temperate or cool climates are preferable. The plants are, however, extremely susceptible to frost. In subtropical regions potatoes are best planted in early autumn, winter or early spring. In temperate climates an early crop can be planted in spring and a late crop planted in midsummer. In cold climates plant in late spring or midsummer so that the plants are fully grown before the onset of cold weather.

Potatoes are tolerant of light or heavy soils but stony or cloddy soils are unsuitable. A deep, well-drained, well-prepared loam with a pH of 5.0–6.5 and ample organic matter is ideal. Select an open position. For crop rotation purposes, choose a site where the soil has been well composted and fertilised for a previous legume or leaf crop.

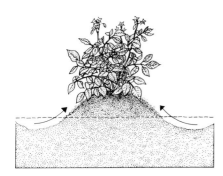

**GROWING POTATOES
HILL UP POTATOES AS TUBERS
DEVELOP.**

Prepare the bed to spade depth prior to planting so that the soil is in friable condition, thereby allowing the tubers to expand evenly. Dig furrows 20 cm deep spaced 80 cm apart. Drizzle in superphosphate or a complete fertiliser with a high phosphate ratio (NPK 5:7:4) at the rate of 5 g to a running metre. Cover the fertiliser with 4 cm of soil.

Tubers for planting should be 30–60 g in weight but large tubers can be cut into pieces provided there is at least one 'eye' or sprout on each piece. Always buy government certified seed potatoes which are harvested from crops free of virus and other diseases. Certified seed potatoes are available from nurseries and garden stores in late winter or early spring. Note that such seed is certified free of diseases upon purchase but there is no guarantee that the crop will not be smitten at some time during growth.

Green the seeds by spreading them thinly in a room with plenty of light but no direct sunlight for 2 to 3 weeks. This process develops a green covering on the pieces, allows the grower to eliminate pieces with weak stems, hastens the emergence of the shoot system and increases yield.

Discard any tubers which develop spindly shoots or other blemishes.

Plant seed pieces 13–15 cm deep at intervals of 30–45 cm. Take care not to injure the shoots which should be facing upwards. Fill in with the remaining soil and rake the bed level. Potato plants will break the surface in about three weeks.

Cultivate between the rows to destroy any weeds which germinate. When the plants are 25 cm high, they should be hilled by drawing the soil up on each side of the plant to give the tubers more room to expand, to smother any weeds and to protect the tubers from the potato moth which can destroy uncovered tubers. Hilling also supports the sprawling stems and prevents greening of tubers formed close to the surface.

Additional fertiliser is seldom necessary but the plants must be watered regularly and thoroughly to promote smooth, well-developed tubers.

Potatoes are ready for digging in 16 to 20 weeks from planting. For small sized 'new' potatoes, start digging when the lower leaves turn yellow — about three weeks after flowering. Potatoes for storage should not be lifted until the plants have died off completely. If left until the plant withers they are longer lasting and less liable to rot.

After removing the soil from the potatoes, discard any showing skin damage or blemishes and store in a cool, airy place which must also be dark to prevent greening. Wooden boxes and cardboard cartons from which light is excluded or thick hessian sacks are good storage containers.

VARIETIES Different varieties of potato have different culinary qualities and should be put to specific uses. Take these differences and personal preferences into account when selecting a variety to grow.

'Sebago' is the most popular white-skinned cultivar and is smooth, oval-shaped and shallow-eyed. It is a good all-rounder. 'Pontiac' is a round potato with thin red skin, white flesh and deep eyes. It is ideal for cooking in the jacket, baked or mashed. For chips or French fries choose from 'Russet Burbank' or 'Kennebec'. 'Kennebec' has white skin and white flesh. 'Bintje' with its cream skin and yellow flesh has excellent flavour and texture, and is useful for dishes where the vegetable is a taste highlight such as potato salad. 'Patrone' with its creamy skin and yellow flesh also suits this purpose well. It is a suitable addition to casseroles but it does not mash smoothly. 'Desiree' is a Dutch variety, oval, pink-skinned with cream, and a delicately textured flesh. It is excellent for baking, roasting and mashing. 'Toolangi Delight' is a dry-textured variety with purplish skin and white flesh useful for mashing, boiling, baking and frying into chips.

Many of these seed potato varieties are now pre-packed and displayed on nursery shelves. Each pack contains information about the specific variety, suggestions for culinary use and detailed cultural information.

Growing Hints

Plant Tubers in spring as soon as seed potatoes are available.
Harvest 16–20 weeks from planting.
Fertilise Apply complete fertiliser high in phosphate during ground preparation.
Planting for Average Family 20–40 plants or sow as many sets as you have room for.
Pests and Diseases Potato moth, aphids, nematodes, leaf roll, mosaic (viruses), Rutherglen bug, 28-spotted ladybird, cutworm, early blight or target spot, Irish or late blight, blackleg, common scab.

JERUSALEM ARTICHOKE IS GROWN FOR ITS EDIBLE TUBERS.

Jerusalem Artichoke (*Helianthus tuberosus*)

ASTERACEAE FAMILY

Jerusalem artichoke is an annual plant growing to a height of 1.5 m with a spread of 1 m. It is grown for its edible tubers. Once established it can be difficult to eradicate so is best confined to an odd corner of the garden which will support little else.

CULTIVATION Tubers are planted like potatoes and are harvested after the plant has flowered and died down in autumn. Not fussy about soil, Jerusalem artichokes nevertheless respond to fertile soil by producing bigger yields. Plant tubers 10–15 cm deep 45 cm apart in rows 1 m apart. They have no specific fertiliser requirements but will respond to a dressing of complete fertiliser.

Growing Hints

Plant Tubers in spring. Harvest autumn.
Fertilise Apply base dressing of complete fertiliser.
Planting for Average Family
3–4 plants.
Pests and Diseases None.

Asian Vegetables

Asian food crops can be grown to perfection in tropical, subtropical and, to a lesser extent, mild temperate climatic zones in Australia. A reasonable portion of the food crop garden can be devoted to cultivating these vegetables in suitable localities. Asian vegetables are basically leaf, root and fruit crops. General cultivation consists of thorough bed preparation to ensure a seedbed of good tilth and sharp drainage combined with good water-holding capacity. Raised beds and applications of animal manure or compost will help to achieve this. Most Asian vegetables will tolerate slightly acidic soil; the ideal pH is between 6.0 and 7.0. All the leaf and root vegetables are best sown directly into the garden, however, the fruiting types can be sown in punnets or peat pots and later transplanted to their permanent positions. Attention to weed management is necessary as Asian vegetables do not compete well with weeds.

The Brassicaceae family is well represented on the Asian vegetable scene, with many different types of cabbage, sprouting broccoli and mustard greens being produced commercially. Brassicas are cool-season crops best grown in spring and autumn. *Brassica narinosa* (broad-backed mustard), *B. alboglabra* (Chinese kale, Gai lum) and *B. parachinensis* (false pak-choy, choy sum) are all used as green vegetables. Bok choy and pe-tsai are the main Chinese cabbage types grown in Australia. For details see pages 48 and 51.

Asian vegetables are fairly tolerant of soil types but they thrive where organic matter has been incorporated. The Chinese root vegetables, like all roots, do not grow well on stony or cloddy soil. They appreciate a light, sandy, well-drained loam to allow for optimum root development. The root vegetables are sensitive to moisture stress and must have adequate and regular watering throughout their development.

Long white radish (loh baak, daikon) is one of the main Asian root crops. It too belongs to the Brassicaceae (mustard) family. It can be eaten raw, cooked or pickled. Its cultivation is identical to the common radish which is also used in Asia. A third type, the leafy radish, is grown as a leaf crop as it has ample foliage but small roots.

Kabu (Japanese turnip) is an erect plant with bulbous roots and short branching stems forming a dense, leafy crown. Both leaves and roots are edible. Small and large varieties are available. This root crop can be grown year round and takes from six to seven weeks to mature from seed. Make spacings 10 cm apart for the small varieties and 20 cm for the large ones.

Other roots to cultivate and harvest to give an oriental touch to cuisine are ginger, taro root and water chestnut. Taro (*Colocasia antiquorum*) is a large-leafed native of tropical Asia and will flourish in the northern regions of Australia. It needs a tropical climate with ample water. The root is prepared and cooked in a similar manner to the potato. Some varieties must be soaked for a period prior to cooking; *C. esculenta* is poisonous if eaten raw. Taro can be grown in rich soil at the edge of a pond, where plants should be spaced 1 m apart. It can also be grown in a garden situation provided adequate water is applied.

The water chestnut is grown and harvested for its crisp corms which are considered to be a delicacy in Southeast Asia. It can be cultivated in a large water-filled container or grown at the edge of a pond. Plant the corms in a large tub then saturate to 20 cm above soil level. The reed-like foliage will grow up to 1 m tall. When it dies down in autumn the tub can be drained and the corms harvested.

Fruiting vegetable crops popular in Asia include the choko, eggplant, hot chilli and okra. For information and full cultural details on these species refer to the main vegetable section. Also cultivated are the fruits of the bitter gourd, Chinese zucchini and luffa.

The angled luffa (*Luffa acutangula*), which is commonly used in Asian cooking, is a fast-growing annual climber with furry leaves and large, oval, deeply fluted fruit. The plant is frost-susceptible so should be planted out at the beginning of the warm season next to a fence or trellis for support. Space plants at 1 m intervals. When the fruits are immature they can be used in stir fries or eaten raw. Once they have reached maturity in about three months, the fibrous fruit skeleton can be used as a body scrubber.

The Chinese zucchini (*Benincasa hispida*) bears a melon-like fruit covered with downy hair and crisp white flesh.

It has a relatively bland taste but is excellent for soup. The plant is a climbing annual with distinctive yellow flowers up to 10 cm across. The flowers may have to be hand-pollinated if pollination does not occur naturally. Plant seeds in spring and summer, spacing at 1 m intervals. A three month growing season is required.

Native to Asia the bitter gourd (bitter melon) is a slender annual climber growing to 2 m high and suited to hot, humid areas. Light, loose, well-drained soil and an open sunny position suit it. The plant is both drought- and frost-susceptible so it is not appropriate for cold areas or

dry inland regions with insufficient rainfall. Sow seeds in spring 50–100 cm apart next to a trellis to give support. The vine will fruit in three months; harvest the long, slender, warty fruit while still immature, hard and green (about 20 cm long). Despite its bitter taste, bitter gourd is an important ingredient in many traditional Asian dishes.

Other vegetables to consider incorporating into the food crop garden for an Asian flavour are shallots, Japanese bunching onion, snow peas and Chinese or garlic chives. Some of the traditional Asian herbs would also be suitable, such as basil, coriander and lemon grass.

IVY HANSEN

ASIAN VEGETABLES ARE BECOMING INCREASINGLY POPULAR AND ARE READILY INCORPORATED INTO A KITCHEN GARDEN. SHOWN HERE ARE TARO, GINGER, LONG WHITE RADISH, BOK CHOY, BITTER MELON AND BABY CHOY SUM.

FRUIT CROPS

Plants whose fruit may be used in desserts or preserves are desirable garden subjects and space for ten or so strawberry plants and a passionfruit vine is not difficult to find. Grow fruits you enjoy eating and varieties that suit the locality.

FRESHLY PICKED FRUITS AND BERRIES RAISED IN THE KITCHEN GARDEN WILL DELIGHT THE GROWER AND COOK ALIKE. SHOWN HERE ARE MELONS, STRAWBERRIES, RASPBERRIES, KIWI FRUIT, PASSIONFRUIT, CAPE GOOSEBERRIES AND ROSELLAS.

Berry Fruits

Cape Gooseberry
(Physalis peruviana)

SOLANACEAE FAMILY

The cape gooseberry is not a true gooseberry but a delicately flavoured little berry borne on a thornless bush which thrives in warm temperate, frost-free regions. It is a native of South America and is both drought- and frost-susceptible. The fruit can be eaten raw or made into jams and conserves. The fruit is a small, yellow, globe-shaped berry enclosed in a papery husk.

CULTIVATION The metre high bushes grow readily in rich, well-drained, friable soil in a hot humid climate where they may be grown as perennials. In warm temperate areas they are grown as annuals and cut down after each crop. Fresh seeds are sown each spring. Provide some shelter from strong winds.

To prepare the bed, work it into a fine tilth adding compost or well-rotted animal manure. Add 5 g of blood and bone or superphosphate per square metre.

Propagation is by seed where this can be obtained. Sow in punnets in spring. When seedlings have been hardened off by gradual exposure to the sun and other elements (approximately 8–10 cm tall) transplant in rows 1 m apart.

Pinch prune to encourage bushy growth and apply water regularly until the fruit sets.

The soft yellow berries are harvested by shaking the bushes to release the fruit from the husks.

VARIETIES 'Golden Gem' ('Golden Nugget').

Gooseberry
(Ribes grossularia)

SAXIFRAGACEAE FAMILY

The gooseberry is the true cold-climate dessert berry and does best growing in cool climates in the southern regions of Australia and New Zealand. It is a deciduous, prickly shrub, growing to 1 m in height and comes in many named varieties.

CULTIVATION Gooseberries thrive in a well-drained, rich soil with added organic matter. They are propagated by hardwood cuttings 30 cm long taken in winter. Remove all lower buds leaving the top four to six buds. Plant the cuttings with the lowest of the remaining buds just above the soil surface. Alternatively, bare-rooted plants may be purchased from nurseries or garden centres.

Growing Hints

Plant Sow seed from mid-September to the end of October in cooler areas. Transplant when seedlings reach 8–10 cm in height.
Harvest 5–6 months.
Fertilise Ensure initial bed preparation of animal manure and blood and bone.
Planting for Average Family 2–3 plants.
Pests and Diseases None.

Growing Hints

Plant For best results plant cuttings by the end of September.
Harvest Spring and summer.
Fertilise Initial generous application of animal manure and blood and bone.
Planting for Average Family 1–2 plants.
Pests and Diseases None.

PROPAGATING AND TRAINING GOOSEBERRIES

WHEN NEW GROWTH SHOWS THAT ROOTS HAVE FORMED, SEVER TIP CUTTING AND TRANSPLANT.
TO CONTROL RAMBLING HABIT OF GOOSEBERRIES, DIVIDE CANES INTO TWO BUNCHES AND TIE TO HORIZONTAL WIRES. PROPAGATE BY PEGGING THE END OF A YOUNG CANE TO THE GROUND.

Plant bushes 80 cm apart. Soil should have an annual application of organic matter plus complete fertiliser. Well cared for gooseberries are long-lived but where bushes need rejuvenating apply sulphate of ammonia in early spring. Prune back lightly each winter.

Ample fruit will be obtained in the first season but subsequent years will give further yields. Fruits must be harvested regularly to keep the bushes bearing over a period of several months in spring and summer.

VARIETIES 'Whinham's Industry' is the best variety for home use.

CAPE GOOSEBERRY THRIVES IN WARM, FROST-FREE REGIONS.

Raspberry
(*Rubus idaeus*)

ROSACEAE FAMILY

Raspberries grow upright canes which are cut out once they have produced fruit in their second year. The bushes sucker freely and need a cool temperate or cold climate to thrive. Raspberries are delicious eaten fresh but are also useful in jams, jellies and desserts where their colour adds brilliance.

CULTIVATION Raspberry plants are both drought- and frost-resistant. The best growing areas are the mountains and tablelands of the southern part of Australia and the South Island of New Zealand.

If planted on slopes with an easterly aspect, protection is obtained from hot westerly winds and afternoon summer sun.

They need a rich soil full of organic matter in a sheltered spot with ample water but adequate drainage, and an annual addition of compost or manure or any chemical fertiliser high in nitrogen.

Plant in rows 1 m apart setting the plants at 75 cm intervals. Alternatively, plant in clumps of three so the plants support each other.

Raspberry canes are biennial and die after they have produced fruit. Pruning consists of cutting out old canes after gathering the berries.

VARIETIES 'Northumberland'; 'Hunter's Perfection'; 'Red Antwerp'; 'Everbearer'; 'Malling Jewel'; 'Malling Promise'; 'Neika'; and 'Willamette'.

Growing Hints

Plant Propagate by cuttings or plant suckers in early winter when dormant.
Harvest From second year onwards.
Fertilise Ensure bed preparation plus annual top dressing of rich manure or compost.
Planting for Average Family 2–3 plants.
Pests and Diseases Anthracnose. They are also subject to the soil-borne Verticillium wilt, and soils in which solanaceous crops (such as tomato, capsicum and eggplant) have been grown are more likely to infect them.

When pruning red raspberries select about half a dozen of the strongest canes and remove others.
With trellised plants, twist half the canes from individual plants through wires on either side and secure them under the canes of the adjoining plant.

Rosella
(*Hibiscus sabdariffa*)

MALVACEAE FAMILY

The fruit of this plant which is related to the hibiscus is used for jams and preserves. It is grown in tropical and subtropical regions and is very ornamental as well as useful with its yellow flowers followed by red or yellow fruit.

CULTIVATION The rosella plant requires a sunny position and manure-enriched soil. Sharp drainage is essential. No special tillage methods are necessary.

Sow seeds after the last frosts to allow six months of warm growing weather. When 15 cm tall transplant seedlings to their permanent positions in rows 1–1.2 m apart spaced at 60 cm intervals within the rows.

To harvest, break off the heads by hand. They should be picked at weekly intervals before the fruit becomes fully mature and woody or stringy.

VARIETIES The common variety has red fruit. There is also a yellowish form.

Growing Hints

Plant Sow seed in spring.
Harvest 9–10 weeks after transplanting; 6–7 weeks from flowering.
Fertilise Prepare manure enriched soil. Do not over-fertilise.
Planting for Average Family 3–4 plants.
Pests and Diseases Relatively free.

Strawberry (*Fragaria* varieties and hybrids)

ROSACEAE FAMILY

Strawberries are among the favourite fruits for the home garden. They are easy to grow, ripen early, do not require much space and, with many cultivars, bear, in a continuing sequence.

IVY HANSEN

ROSELLA FRUITS MAKE DELICIOUS JAMS AND PRESERVES. THE PLANTS ARE EASILY RAISED IN TROPICAL AND SUBTROPICAL CLIMATES.

The plant has a wide climatic tolerance and is grown from the subtropics to regions with a cool to cold winter.

The productive life of the strawberry varies but under favourable conditions beds are usually restocked with a younger planting every two or three years.

CULTIVATION A well-drained bed situated in a sunny position suits strawberries. For this reason as well as for ease of picking, they can be grown in raised beds or planted in barrels or tubs.

Strawberries bear well for three or four seasons so ensure the site is well prepared with compost, animal manure and a complete fertiliser prior to planting. 100 g blood and bone per square metre is very beneficial. Dig over the bed well six to eight weeks before planting.

Soils which are too acidic should be limed a month or so before planting; preferably soil reaction should be slightly acidic to neutral.

Plant runners in late autumn or early spring after removing the outside leaves so that only two or three of the centre leaves and the crown remain. Set the plants by placing the crown just level with the soil; do not bury the crown or leave the roots exposed. Straw or black plastic laid over the soil keeps weeds at a minimum, ensures clean fruit and keeps roots moist. However, if using black plastic, be sure to form a depression in it where the plant comes through so that water is able to run down into the roots rather than lie on top of the plastic.

Where winters are severe late spring frosts can damage the flowers, so in these areas a straw mulch 7–10 cm deep is recommended during frosty periods.

Plants will begin to deteriorate after three or four years, so a new bed should be prepared during autumn and the healthiest plants divided or runners taken to begin the cycle again. While plants are being grown for the fruit, runners should be removed and discarded, but when new stock is needed the healthiest plants should have their flowers removed before setting fruit and be allowed to send out runners for propagation purposes.

When harvesting remember the finest flavour is not attained until the strawberries are fully coloured and ripe. It may be necessary to gather them each day or two during hot weather when they ripen quickly.

VARIETIES Nurseries stock varieties suited to local areas but always check whether they are certified virus-free. 'Torrey' is one of the most popular varieties for temperate areas. 'Cambridge' is recommended for cool and inland districts and 'Red Gauntlet' for warm coastal areas.

Good drainage for strawberries may be obtained by planting them in a bed of soil raised 20 cm above the surrounding area and covered with black plastic. Plant 45 cm apart.

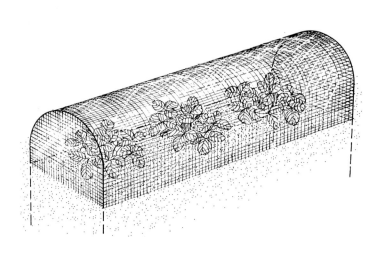

The strawberry is more subject to pests and diseases than other fruit, and not the least pest are birds which will pick off the fruit before it is fully ripe. A fine wire mesh encasing the strawberry bed is almost essential from the time of flowering.

Small cages made of a curve of sparrow netting make the best protection against birds. The ends (and centre if needed) can have long wires which are pushed into the soil.

Growing Hints

Plant Plant runners in late autumn or early spring.
Harvest Summer.
Fertilise Make initial bed preparation with organic matter and complete fertiliser. Upon flowering, use liquid fertiliser every 3–4 weeks.
Planting for Average Family 20 plants.
Pests and Diseases Viruses diseases, leaf spot, grey mould, aphids, birds, snails, slugs, slaters.

The little alpine strawberry is delicious and well worth growing in the home garden. It is a bushy form and does not produce runners. Propagation is by seed. Consult seed clubs or specialist nurseries for availability.

Fruit of the Vine

Kiwi Fruit (Chinese Gooseberry) (*Actinidia chinensis*)

DILLENIACEAE FAMILY

The kiwi fruit is a shrubby, twining, deciduous, vigorously growing vine that is dioecious (with separate male and female plants), and must be grown on some sort of trellis or pergola for support and ease of harvesting.

This plant thrives in mild climates where there are no spring frosts. Moist coastal zones as far as the subtropics and mild inland areas are suitable.

Both a male and female plant are required to produce fruit: one male plant will pollinate up to ten female plants for commercial production. For the home garden, the male scion can be grafted onto the female plant.

CULTIVATION Two methods of propagation are used. With seed male and female seedlings are indistinguishable until they flower, and the fruit types from the female seedlings can be very variable. Alternatively, proven stock can be grafted onto a seedling rootstock.

The stock is then planted about 5 cm deep and each scion should be staked and protected from winds. As the vine is deciduous it can be planted out at any time during the dormant season, either alongside a trellis or a pergola of heavy construction to give the needed support. Regular training and pruning in July will prevent the vigorous vine growth becoming unmanageable and ensure quality yields.

The plant requires a mild climate with adequate moisture. It grows on a wide variety of light, well-drained soils, with added organic matter and some liquid fertiliser as the plant is a heavy feeder. As Kiwi fruit has a shallow root system, the soil must not be allowed to dry out, weed control is very important and only shallow cultivation is possible.

The crop matures in May or June when the fruit is firm enough to handle but not hard. At this time the flesh is an attractive green to whitish colour, fairly firm and juicy with the flavour fully developed.

VARIETIES 'Abbott'; 'Bruno'; 'Hayward'; and 'Monty'. 'Hayward' is the most popular variety despite its tendency to produce smaller yields as it has large-sized, sweet fruit.

Growing Hints

Plant Sow seed in spring or propagate by cuttings or layering in late autumn.
Harvest Late autumn and winter.
Fertilise Monthly feeding with a complete or liquid fertiliser.
Planting for Average Family
2 vines – 1 male and 1 female or male grafted onto female.
Pests and Diseases No serious pests or diseases in the home garden.

Passionfruit (*Passiflora edulis*)

PASSIFLORACEAE FAMILY

Passionfruit is one of the most popular home-grown fruits. The flowers are attractive and make excellent coverage for a pergola, trellis or fence in a sunny spot, provided some support is available for the clinging tendrils.

Passionfruit thrives in the subtropics but also tolerates southern zones in situations where the summer is warm and the winter almost frost free. It can be grown in quite cool regions, provided it is trellised on a warm, sheltered wall where it is protected from the heavy frosts which can occur in open situations. It will also grow in hot inland places but low humidity

IVY HANSEN

KIWI FRUIT IS BOTH AN ORNAMENTAL AND PRODUCTIVE VINE.

during flowering can at times reduce fruit production.

CULTIVATION For home gardens it is best to purchase well-grown plants in pots although the flowers of passionfruit vines are self-fertile and seed is easily gathered and grown from a vine that bears quality crops or from purchased fruit.

The commonly grown purple-flowered species has an average life of three years, so young plants can be propagated at regular intervals as replacements to keep the family well supplied.

Germinate seeds in a warm, sheltered spot in spring using peat pots to avoid disturbing roots when planting out. Place in the permanent position when 15 cm high and the weather is warm. The site for all passionfruits should be well protected from strong winds which reduce crop yields. They will grow in a wide range of soils provided drainage is good; prolonged soggy-soil conditions will lead to root rot. Ideally, the soil should be

---

Growing Hints

Plant Plant year-round avoiding only late autumn and winter. Vines have a life of 3–5 years.
Harvest Vines bear in second year and onwards when grown from seed. Two annual fruiting periods are in spring and late summer.
Fertilise Make bed preparation, an annual dressing of complete fertiliser and a spring boost of sulphate of ammonia or light surface dressing of poultry manure.
Planting for Average Family One mature fruiting vine and a young replacement vine.
Pests and Diseases Woodiness virus which cannot be cured. It spoils the fruit and decreases the vigour of the plant. Destroy diseased plants.

---

slightly acidic, so if it is very acidic, incorporate agricultural lime at least a month prior to planting.

Prepare the spot with some well-rotted animal manure or organic matter, and place a stake in position before planting so that the young vine will have support until the tendrils can attach themselves to the wire frame.

Prune after the fruiting periods to encourage new fruit-bearing arms. Many gardeners do not carry out any pruning of the mature vine. However, if thick laterals are thinned out and the remaining laterals are shortened back to about 40 cm long, fruit size will be improved. Also remove any dead growth. Spring is the time recommended for pruning; if delayed too long, fruit may not mature before winter.

Suitable for cooler areas is the banana passionfruit which can be grown from seed but will not come into fruit as quickly as common passionfruit. It has long, yellow, more acidic fruit than common passionfruit. A vigorous and productive plant, it grows well without too much attention, doing best in humid areas and tolerating much colder weather than *P. edulis*.

VARIETIES Several species can be grown: *Passiflora edulis* (common purple passionfruit); *P. mollisima* (banana passionfruit); *P. antioquiensis* (red-flowered banana passionfruit); and *P. incarnata* (tropical granadilla).

Rockmelon, Honeydew, Cantaloupe (*Cucumis melo*)

CUCURBITACEAE FAMILY

Cucumis melo is a trailing vine with soft roundish leaves and small yellow flowers. *C. m.* var. *cantalupensis* is the cantaloupe with roundish fruit and a hard, rough rind. *C. m.* var. *inodorus*, honeydew, has large, round fruit with smooth rind and green or white flesh while *C. m.* var. *reticulatus*, rockmelon, bears smaller fruit with netted rind and orange flesh.

CULTIVATION Melons are warm season crops adaptable to all climatic

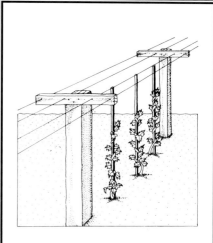

Training Passionfruit

Passionfruit needs a trellis, pergola or open wire fence for support. The granadilla and banana passionfruit do best on a pergola as much of the growth is horizontal. Common passionfruit crops quite well on a vertical trellis.

When training a vine, remove any side shoots which develop from the stem. Pinch the tip from the growing point just below the ultimate height desired, forcing side shoots to develop near the apex.

Vines to be trained on a vertical wire trellis can be allowed to develop side shoots commencing about 25 cm above ground; the side shoots may then be trained to a fan shape.

---

zones. Melons are just big globes of water-filled cells but they can be overwatered. Water is essential in the early stages of growth but the plants rebel against soggy conditions. When plants make too much vine it usually means the soil is too rich in nitrogen. Nipping off leaders generally reverses the effect, throwing energy back into fruit setting.

Sow seed directly into the ground in groups of three or four to a depth of 20 mm in rows 1.5 m apart, each set at 1 m intervals. Seeds will germinate and emerge in six to ten days. Select the strongest seedling to grow on and pull the remainder.

To assess when melons are at their ripest and ready for picking, look for a withered stem and a drum sound when the fruit is rapped.

VARIETIES 'Hayles Best' is the most readily available variety and is resistant to powdery mildew. 'Dixie Jumbo', 'Ambrosia Five Star', 'Supersprint', 'Rocky Ford' and 'Surprise' are also excellent home-garden varieties.

Watermelon (*Citrullus lanatus*)

CUCUBITACEAE FAMILY

Watermelon is a vigorous, annual vine which is frost-sensitive and sun-loving with large fruit varying in size and shape, but generally with red flesh. It is tolerant of most climates excluding inland, cooler coastal and elevated regions.

CULTIVATION While melons require a fairly rich soil, do not over-fertilise with nitrogen as this leads to excessive leafy growth at the expense of fruit.

Watermelon is the most tolerant melon as regards soil pH. Slightly acidic to neutral pH is ideal but watermelon will tolerate soil with a higher acidity.

The seeds will not germinate in cold soil, requiring a soil temperature of at least 15°C preferably more. The watermelon requires a warm, frost-free growing season of at least five months.

Sow seeds in clumps of six, 1.5–3 m apart depending on the variety. Plant seeds pointed end down, 2–3 cm deep; thin seedlings out to the strongest two or three, 20 cm apart.

The plants require ample water as they grow but this should be reduced as the fruit matures. Pinching the terminal tips after the runners have reached 2 m — provided there are sufficient flowers — will reduce the spread of the plants and hasten fruit set. If there are not enough bees in the garden, hand pollinate. The female flowers can be recognised by the immature fruit behind the petals. Transfer the pollen from the male flower with a small paintbrush. Black plastic or hay makes a clean bed for the fruit and also acts as a mulch in keeping down weeds.

Watermelons ripe for harvest will have a flat, dead sound when tapped and the tendrils adjacent to the fruit stem should be dead.

VARIETIES 'Sugar Baby' is recommended for its small size which suits home-grown culture. It bears small round fruit, 4 kg in weight. 'Candy Red Hawkesbury' is the most readily available large-fruited variety.

ROCKMELONS GROW ON LARGE RAMBLING VINES AND REQUIRE AMPLE SPACE TO GROW.

PESTS, DISEASES AND WEEDS

The food-crop gardener has the opportunity to grow fresh and healthy produce for the household, using the minimum amount of chemical interference. Pests, diseases and weeds will, no doubt, have to be dealt with and managed. But by implementing systems of crop rotation, companion planting, early detection of infestations, efficient watering, sensible soil enrichment and fertilising, and organic control methods, spraying with chemicals can be minimised.

RAISED BEDS ARE IDEAL FOR VEGETABLES AS THEY PROVIDE THE SHARP DRAINAGE NECESSARY FOR MOST SPECIES TO THRIVE.

The healthy food-crop garden

Preventative Pest Management

When dealing with garden pests and diseases, there are some preventative measures which can be implemented to minimise infestations, thereby reducing the need to resort to chemical control measures. Prevention is always better than cure.

Vigorous, well-grown vegetables will withstand attacks by diseases and pests better than those which are struggling to grow. Watering should be thorough; deep enough to ensure soil is at field capacity but not waterlogged. Drip irrigation rather than overhead sprinkling should be considered. Applying adequate nutrients is also important in order to grow vegetables quickly.

Regular inspection of vegetable crops is essential to detect the first signs of a disease or pest and to start control measures promptly before the problem gets out of hand.

Strict garden hygiene practices should be implemented. Many diseases and pests can survive on neighbouring plants, weeds, plant refuse or rubbish. Clear weeds, long grass and trash from the surrounds of the garden. Clean cultivation and early disposal of spent crops will break the life cycle of diseases and pests. Plants severely affected by either should be destroyed by burning. Do not compost these plants as the organisms they harbour may carry over to reinfect in the future.

Monoculture, or the continual growing of the same crop on the same ground, encourages the rapid proliferation of disease organisms and pests peculiar to that plant family. Crop rotation in the vegetable garden will help prevent the carry-over of diseases and pests.

Classification of Pests

CHEWING PREDATORS

Some of the worst garden pests belong in this group which includes all caterpillars and grubs, cutworms and snails, beetles, grasshoppers, crickets and slaters. They cause damage to leaves, stems, flower buds and fruits.

Dipel bio-insecticide is particularly effective against caterpillars and has no poisonous effects on other living creatures.

Contact sprays or stomach poisons will kill them but all parts of the plant must be saturated with the solution. The withholding period must be long enough for the spray to lose its toxic effect on humans.

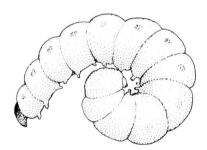

CUTWORM LAVA IS A CHEWING PREDATOR WHICH CAN BE CONTROLLED BY DIPEL.

SUCKING INSECTS

Aphids, jassids, white fly, thrips, shield bugs and mealie bugs belong to this category. These insects use a proboscis like a hypodermic syringe to remove sap from plant tissue thereby causing collapse of cells and wilting. They usually occur in plagues and are

WEEDS COMPETE WITH VEGETABLES FOR MOISTURE AND NUTRIENTS.

IVY HANSEN

APHIDS ARE SAP-SUCKING INSECTS OCCURRING IN PLAGUE PROPORT-IONS. USE COMPANION PLANTING TECHNIQUES OR CHEMICAL SPRAYS TO REDUCE INFESTATIONS.

susceptible to contact insecticides and systemic chemical sprays which poison the sap they suck. Once again an interval between spraying and harvesting is necessary.

BURROWING PESTS

Maggots, leaf miners, flies, fruit fly larvae, and coddling moth lavae fall into this group. Spray with Rogor or destroy affected fruit and plants.

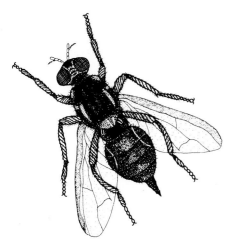

FRUIT FLY LAY EGGS IN PARTLY GROWN FRUIT.

FUNGAL DISEASES

Fungal diseases can be carried in seed, soil or on other plants. Fusarium wilt is a common fungal disease frequently found on tomato plants. Mildew on cucurbits is caused by a fungal disease; others are various forms of blight and rust. These diseases are often present in the soil and are easily transmitted by sucking and chewing insects and gardening tools. Fungal spores can be

wind-borne but are also spread by rain splash or overhead watering. Fungal diseases are more active in warm, humid weather.

In extreme cases soil may have to be disinfected, but total eradication of fungi is difficult because of the ease with which spores are transmitted. Seed can be treated with fungicides prior to sowing or plants can be dusted with fungicide as they grow.

VIRUS DISEASES

Virus diseases can be quite serious in beans, carrot, lettuce, potato and tomato. Viruses are transmitted by sap-sucking insects such as mites, aphids and thrips. Control of these pests gives control over virus diseases in many cases. There is no spray to control virus diseases themselves and the only remedy is to remove and burn infected plants. Good hygiene is most important.

Chemical Sprays

If chemical sprays are the only answer, you will find a great number available. Some are biological control sprays, some are specific against certain organisms, while others are 'broad spectrum' which control many. Certain chemicals are safer to use in the vegetable garden because they have a low residual action and degrade quickly into harmless compounds. The withholding period, which is the number of days from spraying (or dusting) to harvesting, is a guide to their safety. The best chemicals to use are those with a short withholding period (seven days or less).

Malathion (seven days) is a contact insecticide which controls aphids, beetles, bugs, caterpillars, cutworms, jassids, thrips and white fly. Carbaryl (three days) controls beetles, bugs, caterpillars and cutworms. Derris (three days) controls beetles and caterpillars. Pyrethrum (one day) controls aphids, caterpillars, jassids and thrips. Rogor (seven days) will control

To minimise the need for spraying with pesticides, fungicides and insecticides:
• eradicate weeds which shelter pests;
• rotate crops; and
• try organic sprays.
• Consider the birds, bees, fish and animals, as well as humans by using toxic chemicals only when absolutely necessary.

all sap-sucking insects and fruit fly. Kelthane (or Dicofol) (seven days) is a specific chemical for the control of red spider and mites.

Zineb (seven days) is an all-purpose fungicide which will control most vegetable diseases (including downy mildew and rust) but not powdery mildew. Benlate (five days) is a systemic fungicide for the control of powdery mildew and many other diseases but it will not control downy mildew or rust. Copper oxychloride and Dry Bordeaux (one day) will control leaf spot, leaf blight, downy mildew and rust. Karathane (or Dinocap) (three weeks) is a specific fungicide to control powdery mildew. To prevent damping off disease, dust seeds or spray seedlings with Zineb or Dry Bordeaux which are wettable powders.

SAFETY PRECAUTIONS

Dusts and sprays can be used with greater safety if the following precautions are taken.
1 Read directions carefully before using.
2 Do not use higher concentrations than are recommended.
3 Do not mix different sprays together unless it is stated that it is safe to do so.
4 Do not inhale fumes from dusts or sprays.

5 Avoid contact of dusts or sprays with skin.

6 Do not spray in windy or wet weather.

7 Do not spray in the heat of the day.

8 Do not smoke or eat when dusting or spraying.

9 Rinse and wash sprayer, buckets and mixing gear with detergent before storing.

10 After dusting or spraying, wash face and hands thoroughly.

11 Store dusts and sprays away from children or in a locked cupboard.

12 Do not store unused 'made up' sprays.

13 Observe the withholding period between application and harvest strictly, and wash vegetables thoroughly before eating raw or before cooking.

Toxic sprays have been available for many years and along with their proliferation has grown a careless disregard for their harmful effects. Responsible gardeners should be aware of the harm done to the atmosphere and to the soil by chemical treatments, and be inventive in the use of alternatives and organic methods.

Organic Alternatives

The advantages of using organic methods of pest and disease control are that it is kinder to the environment and the number of predatory, helpful insects will build up which may prove more worthwhile in removing unwanted pests and diseases than chemical methods in the long run.

Many sprays — onion, garlic, chilli, marigold, nasturtium, turnip, parsnip, rhubarb leaf, or soap flake — repel pests by an offensive taste or smell. Pyrethrum and derris sprays are sometimes used, and sulphur and copper compounds.

SOAP SPRAY

Mix 56 g of soap flakes or grated pure soap with 5 litres of hot water and allow to cool. This is useful against some caterpillars and other larvae.

GARLIC SPRAYS

90 g chopped garlic cloves
2 tablespoons mineral oil or liquid paraffin
15 g of pure soap or soap flakes
500 mL warm water

Mix garlic and oil and stand for 48 hours. Dissolve grated soap or flakes in warm water. Mix two solutions together and strain. A strong solution of one part mixture to 50 parts water can be used. Useful against sucking insects and caterpillars. Spray all parts of the plant, under and over leaves.

A stronger spray can be made by adding several crushed chillies and several minced onions (pungency is the aim) to several crushed garlic nobs. To each 500 g of matter add 1 litre of hot water. Cover and leave 48 hours. Strain, then add 1 litre of cold water and 2 teaspoons of detergent. Use as a general pesticide by mixing one part to two parts of water.

RHUBARB SPRAY

½ kg rhubarb leaves
1 L water

Boil leaves in water for half an hour. Dilute mixture with 4.5 litres water and use within a day of making. This spray is useful against aphids on roses and is safe for bees. Note that this is a very poisonous mixture and fruit and vegetables should not be eaten after spraying for at least two days. Soft soap can be added to a rhubarb spray.

QUASSIA SPRAY

28 g quassia chips
1 L water

Mix for half an hour. Strain and add 28 g soft soap. Dilute with three parts water to one part of solution. You can use this spray against aphids and small caterpillars. It will kill hover fly larvae but not ladybirds and their larvae or bees.

Weed Management

To reduce the necessity for chemical weed control introduce hygienic practices into the food crop garden. Be prepared initially to try to eradicate weeds by hand or by surface cultivation.

Tilling the top several centimetres of soil about plant rows on hot sunny days reduces weeds which compete with vegetables while thriving on expensive soil amendments. Weed seeds have greater viability than most crop seeds and may lie in the soil from season to season awaiting the right conditions for germinating. Therefore, weed

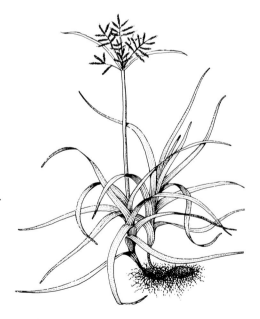

NUT GRASS HAS A TOUGH RHIZATOMOUS ROOT AND SHOULD BE EXCLUDED FROM COMPOST MAKING.

Pest and disease control chart

Note: Chemicals stated as being controls are those known to be effective but are not by any means the only, or necessarily the best pesticides, fungicides, miticides or insecticides to tackle the job. There are too many to include them all in this table.

PEST OR DISEASE V = Virus B = Bacteria F = Fungus	DESCRIPTION	PLANTS AFFECTED	ACTION INCLUDING CHEMICAL CONTROL WITH NAMED PROPRIETARY BRAND. *ALWAYS OBSERVE WITHHOLDING PERIOD.*
Anthracnose (F)	Small reddish-brown, slightly sunken spots on pods growing to dark areas 6 mm across. Stem and leaves spotted, veins blackened.	Beans, vine crops	Burn infected plants; spray remainder with Bordeaux; do not save seed for sowing.
Aphids (various species)	Affected foliage distorted. Sucking insects massing on new growth resulting in sooty mould on growing tips or leaves. May be green, brown, black or grey.	Beans, brassicas, sweet corn	Malathion or Rogor.
Bacterial soft rot (B)	Found in decaying vegetable matter in the soil. Worse in hot weather. Produces mushy decay of leaf petioles near the ground.	Bok choy	Destroy diseased crops; Practise crop rotation.
Black beetle	Shiny black burrowing beetle 12 mm long. Larval stage also active depredator. Young plants attacked just below soil causing wilting and death.	Leafy vegetables, corn, potato, tomato	Bugmaster or Malathion.
Blackleg (B)	Rotting of tubers accompanied by offensive odour. Blackening at base of shoot.	Radish, potato, turnip, cabbage	Remove and destroy plants; practise crop rotation; obtain seed from reputable source.
Blight (F)	Early blight or target spot on tomatoes. Irish blight on potatoes. Late varieties typified by moulding and discolouration of leaves. Affects tubers.	Tomato, potato	Zineb or Mancozeb.
Blossom end rot	Brownish sunken area at flower-end related to lack of calcium in soil.	Tomato	Apply calcium carbonate before planting; water regularly and mulch soil.
Botrytis (F) Grey mould	Brown mass of fungal spores causing rotting, often covered by a grey furry growth.	Strawberry	Benlate.
Cabbage moth and white butterfly	White butterfly caterpillars are velvety green with indistinct yellowish stripe on backs and sides. Cabbage moth caterpillars are bright green and wriggle or drop off leaf if disturbed. Both caterpillars decimate plants through to the heart.	Brassicas	Dipel bio-insecticide or Derris Dust.

PEST OR DISEASE V = Virus B = Bacteria F = Fungus	DESCRIPTION	PLANTS AFFECTED	ACTION INCLUDING CHEMICAL CONTROL WITH NAMED PROPRIETARY BRAND. *ALWAYS OBSERVE WITHHOLDING PERIOD.*
Caterpillars and loopers	Large, soft, green grubs.	Most green leaf crops	Dipel, Derris Dust or Carbaryl.
Club root (F)	Grossly distorted roots with swellings. Can cause stunting and wilting of aboveground parts of plant.	Brassicas	Sterilise soil; increase soil pH; rotate crops; drain soil.
Cutworms	Fawn grubs to 4 cm long. Invade at night, chew young plants at ground level.	Cabbage, beans, peas, lettuce, tomato, potato	Spray soil at base of plant with Carbaryl.
Corn earworm	Caterpillar of the heliothis moth which lays its eggs on corn silks.	Corn	Cut ear tips after pollination when silks have turned brown and begun to dry.
Damping off (F)	Seedlings attacked at ground level and topple over.	Seedlings of various vegetables	Use resistant varieties; dust seeds with fungicide prior to sowing.
Downy mildew (F)	Yellow-black fungus patches on leaves, white down on lower surface finally killing foliage.	Cucurbits, beetroot, onion, capsicum, rhubarb	Bordeaux mixture; burn affected parts.
Earth mites	1 mm long, black body, red legs. Winter pests.	Silver beet, peas, lettuce, turnip	Establish hygienic practices through weed control.
Fruit fly	Small fly, lays eggs in partly grown fruit.	Tomato, eggplant, capsicum	Rogor; collect and destroy affected fruit.
Fusarium root rot (F)	Base of stem and main roots become reddish, then roots rot.	Beans	Benlate; rotate crops; use resistant varieties.
Fusarium wilt (F)	Wilting and yellowing, withering from bottom upwards.	Tomato, melon, squash, marrow	Benlate; rotate crops; use resistant varieties.
Green vegetable bug	Adult is bright green, shield-like sucking insect causing distortion and wilting of leaves, blotches on tomatoes (fruit) and beans (pods).	Tomato	Carbaryl or Malathion.
Halo blight (B)	Carried by seed. Brown spots on leaves with wide yellowish border. Defoliates plants which die.	Beans	Practise rotation; buy seed from a reliable source; destroy infected plants.
Leaf miner	Minute insect whose larvae tunnel between surfaces of leaf.	Silver beet	Burn infected leaves; Rogor.
Leaf roll (V)	Leaves thicken, roll at margins, stiffen and become vertical. Tuber yield small.	Potato	Avoid potatoes with spindly shoots.
Leaf spot (F)	Different fungi cause spotting on leaves.	Various vegetables and strawberry	Zineb; spray with copper oxychloride; where practicable remove and burn affected leaves on silver beet and encourage new growth.

PEST OR DISEASE V = Virus B = Bacteria F = Fungus	DESCRIPTION	PLANTS AFFECTED	ACTION INCLUDING CHEMICAL CONTROL WITH NAMED PROPRIETARY BRAND. *ALWAYS OBSERVE WITHHOLDING PERIOD.*
Mosaic (V)	Mottled greenish-yellow leaves. Spread by aphids.	Potato	Control aphids with Malathion or Rogor.
Neckrot (F)	Grey mould on neck of onion.	Onion in storage	Harvest bulbs only when tops have died down; air in a dry shed rather than outdoors.
Necrotic yellows (V)	Virus causing leaf stunt and yellowing, often making leaves lopsided.	Lettuce	Control aphids, weed out any milk thistles which harbour disease.
Nematodes (Eel worms)	Microscopic thread-like soil organisms causing swollen galls on roots. Most prolific in sandy soil.	Root crops	Burn diseased plants; fumigate soil with a nematicide such as Nemacur.
Onion maggot	Tunnels into stems of seedlings which wilt and die.	Onion, beans, brassicas, cucurbits	Do not apply blood and bone or animal manure close to planting time.
Potato moth	Brownish-grey with a wingspan of 1.3 cm. Flies about at dusk. Small pinky grey larvae attack leaves and tubers. Tunnelling larvae invade leaves and tubers.	Potato	Carbaryl; to prevent keep plants well hilled up and covered when lifted.
Powdery mildew (F)	White or pale grey talcum-soft fungus which covers all parts of the plant. Eventually leaves turn black and fall off.	Cucurbits, parsnip	Use resistant varieties; remove affected leaves; use wettable sulphur spray.
Pumpkin beetle	Orange-yellow beetle with four black spots. Eats seedlings and young fruit.	Most cucurbits	Carbaryl.
Red spider	Sap-sucking red mite which clusters under leaves, causing mottling and defoliation. Most serious in dry weather.	Legume and cucurbit crops	Rogor; burn old infested plants.
Ring spot (F)	Prevalent in cool, moist conditions. 1 cm spots, either yellowish-brown, dark grey or black.	Cabbage, cauliflower, broccoli	Practise crop rotation; buy disease-free seed; remove and destroy all diseased plant parts.
Root rot (F)	Plants become stunted, foliage wilts and yellows, roots become discoloured and rot.	Beans, peas, potato	Burn diseased plants; use disease-free seed.
Rust (F)	Raised spots of reddish brown spores on underside of leaves.	Beans	Zineb or Mancozeb.
Rutherglen bug	Small, grey sucking insect, moves quickly and flies off if disturbed; causes wilting in young leaves, may kill plant.	Potato, tomato, silver beet	Malathion.
Snails and slugs	More prolific in wet weather.	Seedlings and all tender growth of plants	Metaldehyde baits.

PEST OR DISEASE V = Virus B = Bacteria F = Fungus	DESCRIPTION	PLANTS AFFECTED	ACTION INCLUDING CHEMICAL CONTROL WITH NAMED PROPRIETARY BRAND. ALWAYS OBSERVE WITHHOLDING PERIOD.
Spider mites	Suck sap from underside of leaves turning leaves yellow and mottled.	Eggplant, beans	Establish hygienic practices of clearing weeds and dead plant material; practise crop rotation.
Target spot (F)	*See* Early blight.	Tomato	Zineb.
Thrips	Minute grey sucking insects; cause silvering and distortion of leaves. Warm damp weather favours them.	Onion	Rogor.
Tomato mite and Tomato caterpillar	Mite attacks stems; leaves shrivel and die from the bottom of the plant up. Caterpillar attacks buds and fruit.	Tomato, potato, eggplant	Control mites with wettable sulphur or sulphur dust; spray with Rogor from seedling stage to control caterpillars.
28-spotted ladybird (leaf eating)	Small orange beetle with 28 black spots. Both adult and larvae feed on upper surface of leaves which become skeletonised.	Potato, tomato, cucurbits	Carbaryl or Malathion.
Vegetable weevil	Grey-brown weevil up to 13 mm long, grubs usually green or yellow. Both stages are night-time depredators above and below ground.	All root crops, tomato and brassicas	Malathion; spray plants and ground with Carbaryl.
White rot (F)	Soil-borne fungus attacks roots and base of bulb. White cotton-like growth. Leaves yellow and die back.	Onion family	Practise crop rotation; burn diseased plants; use seeds rather than seedlings.
White rust (F)	Mass of small, white, circular raised spots on both sides of the leaves. Prevalent in cool, wet weather.	Bok choy and other brassicas	Destroy diseased crops; practise crop rotation.
Wilts (B)	Leaves become limp, turn yellow or brown and drop off. Prevalent during dry spells.	Tomato, eggplant, capsicum, broad beans, raspberry	Disinfect soil; rotate crops; use certified seed.

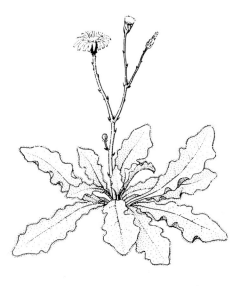

management will be a seasonal routine rather than a one-off task.

Weeding then leaving the bed to lie fallow until a second crop of weeds surfaces and re-weeding is a useful method. Solarisation during hot weather is also effective. This involves covering the food crop bed with plastic and allowing the soil beneath to heat up to such a degree as to kill any weeds and weed seeds. Several hot days are

ENDEAVOUR TO ERADICATE WEEDS LIKE CAT'S EAR BY HAND BEFORE RESORTING TO CHEMICAL CONTROLS.

needed to heat the bed to the required 60°C to kill the plant material.

Do not use weeds which propagate from nodes and root sections in compost stacks. Especially, do not leave weeds of this kind lying around after pulling them from the soil. If they cannot be burnt put them in the rubbish bin. Pulled weeds used as a mulch around small plants will revive as the plants are watered.

Using drip or trickle irrigation watering systems will ensure your food crops are given adequate water while unwanted weeds out of the area are

SUBTERRANEAN CLOVER MAY BE DUG OUT AND COMPOSTED.

starved of moisture and are therefore unlikely to thrive or spread.

Weeds capable of rapid regrowth should be burned, a sure way of destroying them. Use the ashes in your garden as potash. The need to use chemical weedicides can be further minimised by:

- weeding routines;
- preventing seed development;
- digging in weed crops; and
- mulching the food crop garden.

Using Chemicals

The many garden spray compounds and dusts available to the food crop gardener are often highly poisonous, but because weed pests such as couch grass, kikuyu, nut grass, onion weed, oxalis, dock and dandelion are so difficult to eradicate by hand, a gardener must often resort to a herbicide.

Cleaning new ground with the use of weed sprays will give the gardener an unhindered start, but a new crop of weeds can appear within days of spraying and gardeners sometimes become 'hooked' on herbicides under the impression they must win the battle if it goes on long enough. Weeds and pests, however, develop physiological and genetic resistance to sprays and may come back sturdier and more rampant than before.

The chemical war is never really won but proper management techniques should reduce the necessity for spraying at frequent intervals.

When choosing a weedicide, look for one which will kill as many different types of weeds as possible so that you are not obliged to buy a number of costly sprays, but take care when using these wide-spectrum sprays that drift does not affect your food crops.

Also consider the term of residual effect when choosing a weedicide. A product with a short-term residual effect should be preferred over a long-term one. Zero or Roundup are probably two of the safest sprays to use and are based on gylphosate. The hormone sprays 2,4-D amine and MCPA are notoriously effective but particularly dangerous.

The finer the spray nozzle, the further spray drift will travel. Drift has

ONION WEED IS DIFFICULT TO ERADICATE. CHEMICALS MAY HAVE TO BE RESORTED TO.

been identified kilometres away from the place where it was applied. Spray close to the subject and use a shield over the nozzle (easily fabricated by making a hole in the bottom of a bucket, bowl or plastic bottle) to direct the spray more accurately. Observe all safety rules suggested on the containers, and for your own protection always use a face mask to avoid breathing in toxic fumes.

Spray only tenacious weeds. Hoe out young paspalum, purslane, mallow, plantain and dock. It is most important to spray before seed heads develop on the plant.

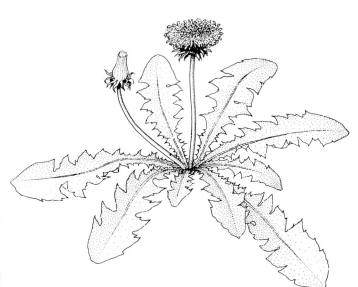

DANDELION HAS AN INVASIVE HABIT IN GARDENS.

OXALIS HAS PERSISTENT CORMS AND SHOULD BE REMOVED AND DESTROYED.